Barcelona

Part of the Langenscheidt Publishing Group

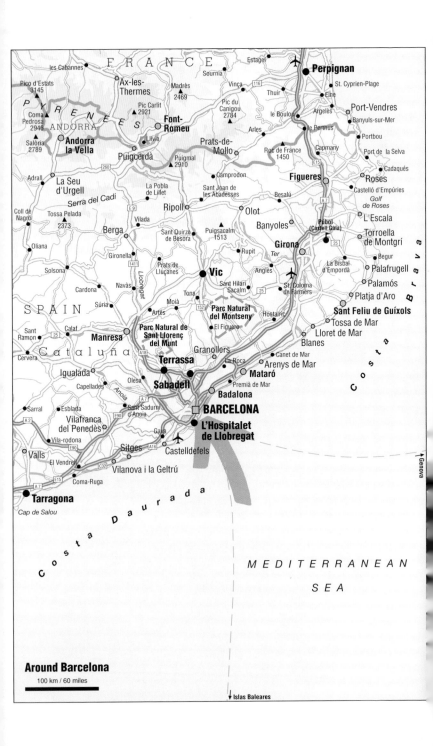

Around Barcelona

100 km / 60 miles

Welcome

This guidebook combines the interests and enthusiasms of two of the world's best-known information providers: Insight Guides, who have set the standard for visual travel guides since 1970, and Discovery Channel, the world's premier source of non-fiction television programming.

Its aim is to help visitors get the most out of the city during a short stay, and to this end Insight Guides' Barcelona expert, Roger Williams, has created a series of carefully crafted itineraries. The longer tours link the essential sights of La Rambla and the Barri Gòtic, Montjuïc and the waterfront, and the Eixample, with its *modernista* architecture and Gaudí's unfinished cathedral; shorter options explore other interesting areas and some lesser-known aspects of the city; and four excursions take in the beach at Sitges, the Holy Mountain of Montserrat, the wine towns of Penedès and the Dalí museums. Supporting the itineraries are sections on history and culture, eating out, shopping, nightlife and practical information. The book is continually updated with the invaluable help of Judy Thomson, a resident of Barcelona

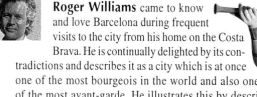

Roger Williams came to know and love Barcelona during frequent visits to the city from his home on the Costa Brava. He is continually delighted by its contradictions and describes it as a city which is at once one of the most bourgeois in the world and also one of the most avant-garde. He illustrates this by describing a scene he witnessed during the rush-hour one morning on La Rambla: 'Walking towards me was a man in a grey jacket, shirt and tie with a briefcase under his arm. His haircut was trim, a little grey at the temples. He was as middle aged and middle class as me, but as he passed I looked down and noticed his short tight blue skirt. Only in Barcelona, I thought.'

HISTORY AND CULTURE

The city of Columbus and Gaudí, the hub of Catalan nationalism, the impact of the 1992 Olympic Games, and subsequent urban regeneration – a look at forces, personalities and events that have shaped Barcelona **11**

ITINERARIES

Pages 2/3: Casa Batlló's sinuous facade
Pages 8/9: the triumphant return of Columbus

BARC

History &Culture

Barcelona is the capital of the richest region in Spain, with all the amenities you would expect to find in a great metropolis. It has over the centuries been the cradle of both mercantile and industrial Spain. People from other parts of the country have come here to Catalonia find work and many *barcelonins* have seen themselves as separate from what they regard as in-dolent Spain supported by the taxes they pay to Madrid. It has been this sense of injustice, combined with a sobriety, a belief in hard work and an unshakeable faith in themselves and their culture that has driven the Cata-lan *barcelonin* forwards. It may not have always been a winning formula, but it is certainly a formidable one, for with it a culture and a language, against enormous odds, have managed to survive very successfully.

The history of the city and of Catalonia, the region of northeast Spain which Madrid has once more allowed a degree of self-control, is a stormy one, with high crests overshadowing deep long troughs. Always its own man, Catalonia has sided with Muslim against Christian, French against Spaniard, anarchist against fascist.

Carthaginians, Romans and Moors

The ancients did not rate this town site too highly. It had a prominent look-out hill in Montjuïc, and a harbour of sorts, but it was not a greatly fought-over haven. The Iberians had a settlement here and Hamilcar Barca, father of Hannibal, is said to have given it its name as he advanced his Carthaginian armies up from Africa towards his hated Rome. The retaliating Romans made their regional capital at Tarragona down the coast. In Barcelona they erected a temple to Jupiter on Montjuïc, and built city walls, with 78 towers, against which the royal palace complex leans. The 12ha (30-acre) town was centred on Mont Tàber, a high spot where the cathedral stands; their forum was in Plaça Sant Jaume, and inside the entrance to the nearby Centre d'-Excursionistes de Catalunya in Carrer Paradís are columns of a Temple of Augustus. The busy Roman city streets can be glimpsd in excavations beneath the Museu d'Història de la Ciutat.

The Visigoths stepped into the vacuum which was left when the Romans departed. Their chief Athaulf seized the city 'with his best men' and he was later assassinated here, but their architectural legacy is minimal. Nor did the Moors who followed them leave their mark physically, culturally or, more impor-tantly, linguistically, as they did in the rest of Spain. After 85 years they were seen off by the Franks under Charlemagne. It was Charlemagne,

Left: painted ladies on an altar urn
Right: Wilfred the Hairy, founder of the House of Barcelona

making a buffer state of dependent counties along his southwestern flank, who gave Barcelona its independence, in the 9th century. The first Count of Barcelona to receive a degree of autonomy was Guifré el Pilós (Wilfred the Hairy), who, in a series of campaigns during the 870s, consolidated the counties of northern Catalonia and began the House of Barcelona, a dynasty which continued in an unbroken line for 500 years.

The Boom Begins

The expansion of the cathedral chapters is an indication of the city's early growth – by 1005 there were 17 of them and the canons were fast gaining a reputation for erudition. But Barcelona was not rich in learning alone: the profits of war and the agricultural produce of the surrounding plains made the town materially wealthy, and by the 1070s most of the transactions of the city were made in gold. Some of this money was invested in maritime enterprises: trade was good, a city fleet was established and the word 'Catalan' appeared in documents for the first time. Under Ramón Berenguer III, who reigned from 1082 to 1131, and whose statue stands outside the Royal Chapel in Via Laietana, Provence in France was acquired by marriage and the Moors were ejected from Tarragona and pushed back beyond the Ebro river.

Over the next two centuries the city rode high. In 1160 a contemporary account records that there were ships from 'Pisa, Genoa, Sicily, Greece, Alexandria and Asia' moored off Barcelona. In the same year Ramón Berenguer IV gave permission for new public baths to be built outside the city wall – today the Carrer dels Banys Nous, the Street of the New Baths. In 1162 Barcelona teamed up with the crown of Aragon, its landlocked inland neighbour, to form the confederation of the count-kings of Catalonia-Aragon.

In 1229 Jaume I, The Conqueror, embarked on a naval expansion which was to swallow up the Balearic islands, Sardinia and Sicily and reach for Greece. At home he knocked down the old city walls and built new ones ten times as long. Up until the 19th century these walls, which contain the Barri Gòtic area, defined the old town. Inland they ran north from Plaça de Catalunya to Passeig Lluís Companys, then down to the sea passing through Ciutadella Park. On the southern side they followed the left bank of the Riera d'en Malla, an intermittent river that ran from the Collserola hills to the sea. This was the *rambla*, the dried-up river bed that became the modern city's exciting thoroughfare.

By the 14th century Catalonia was one of the Mediterranean's most formidable maritime nations and its rule book, the *Consolat de Mar*, governed trade throughout the sea. The 14th century turned the town into a clamorous dustbowl, the Gothic city rose up, riding roughshod over the existing Romanesque: the cathedral, Santa María del Pi, Santa María del Mar, the Royal Palace's Saló de Tinell, the town hall's Saló del Consell de Cent, the trading hall of La Llotja and the great aisles of the Drassanes shipyards, which now house the Maritime Museum.

Left: statue of Ramón Berenguer III outside the Royal Chapel

history/culture

Even the ravages of the Black Death in the middle of the century did not shatter the city's self confidence or put an end to the building boom.

Unlike much of Spain, Barcelona is not a city of nobles and counts. The tombstones in the cathedral cloisters attest to that. The luminaries buried here are merchants and guildsmen: each one had to buy his slab. The aristocrats of this merchant city favoured the Ribera district in the streets behind the dockside trading hall. The wealthy paid for the building of Santa María del Mar here and they built their mansions and palaces in Carrer de Montcada, several of which now house the Picasso Museum.

The arts were well patronised, and in 1395 annual competitions for poets and troubadors, called the Jocs Florals, were initiated. They were based on a similar event in Toulouse, for Catalonia, which then extended over the Pyrenees into the Roussillon in France, had close links with its neighbour, Languedoc. Their languages were almost the same.

City of Columbus

The year 1992 was not just an important date for Barcelona because of the Olympics. It was also the 500th anniversary of Columbus's discovery of America and the expulsion of the Moors from Spain. It was not in fact until 1493 that Columbus – Cristobal Colom – returned in triumph to Barcelona,

to be received by Ferdinand and Isabella in the Saló de Tinell in the Royal Palace. The Genoese navigator, whose statue stands on a great plinth at the foot of La Rambla, did Barcelona little good with his discovery. Seville was the city granted the right to trade with the New World and Barcelona suffered economic decline.

Ferdinand was the end of the Catalonia-Aragon line. When he married Isabella of Castile in 1469 the peninsula became united under one rule. Their daughter married Philip of Austria and thereby introduced the Habsburgs to Spain. From that time onwards, Barcelona was to be in constant conflict with the central government, determined to keep its identity, its laws and its customs.

During the Thirty Years' War with France, which began in 1639, Barcelona was less than enthusiastic about supplying arms, men and money to Madrid. As a result mercenary troops were billeted on Catalonia and a viceroy was appointed to keep an eye on the city. Catalonia then declared itself a republic and formed an alliance with the French king, Louis XIII. Not surprisingly, reaction from Madrid was swift. Barcelona was besieged and eventually defeated in 1651. It was allowed to keep its constitution, its *Usatges*, but in the Treaty of the Pyrenees that concluded the war in 1659 all Catalonia north of the Pyrenees was ceded to France.

Above: Ferdinand of Aragon, whose marriage to Isabella of Castile united Spain under one rule

Barcelona could not get away with bucking Madrid again. When Carlos II died without an heir in 1700, a war of succession broke out. The Austrian Habsburg line was favoured by Barcelona, backed by England and Genoa. But the House of Bourbon put up Felipe V who was installed on the throne in the Peace of Utrecht in 1713. His troops captured Barcelona after a 13-month siege and entered the city on 11 September, now remembered as La Diada, Catalonia's national day. Revenge was dramatic. All Barcelona's privileges and separate laws were abolished. Books were burned, Catalan banned from official use, the whole of La Ribera district was destroyed and the University, which stood beside the Rambla Estudis, was turned into a barracks.

Industrial Expansion

When the trade ban with the Americas was lifted in 1778, cotton began to arrive, and as the 19th century got underway so did the industrial revolution. The first steamship left the harbour in 1836; 12 years later Spain's first

railway linked Barcelona to the nearby town of Mataró; and in 1842 gas light first illuminated the city. Much of the industry was settled on the north side of the town, in Poble Nou, and huge textile manufacturing centres grew up just inland, at Terrassa and Sabadell. Barcelona itself reached bursting point and the old city wall just had to come down.

In 1859 the plans of the architect Ildefons Cerdà were chosen as a blueprint for the whole of the new city, to be called the Eixample (Extension), spreading inland from the Plaça de Catalunya. Keeping to a grid system, the blocks of houses lined the wide boulevards. The biggest, the Gran Via de les Corts Catalanes, cuts the city in half and today allows a driver to go straight through, south to north, without turning left or right. Many of the city's monasteries were dissolved and pulled down, which is how the Liceu theatre and the Palau de la Música Catalana found their sites.

The new building gave great scope for architects and designers. Their patrons were industrialists such as Eusebi Güell and the emerging bourgeoisie, and a new spirit of national identity began to take a grip. It was a rebirth, the Renaixença, and it was not confined to any one class or political set. The Jocs Florals were revived and the Catalan language, only handed down orally since the Bourbons' decree, was written and published once more. This cultural rediscovery burst on to the world stage in 1887 when it

Above: a painting by Ramón Casas, the most representative of the Modernista artists who flourished at the end of the 19th century

was suddenly decided to hold a Universal Exhibition in Ciutadella Park the following year. The exhibition triggered the Modernisme movement, Barcelona's version of art nouveau.

Increasing prosperity encouraged Barcelona to look down on Madrid even more. This prosperity was not all of its own making: its products were sold in the protected markets of Spain's American colonies, and there was an outcry in Barcelona when these colonies were lost at the end of the 19th century. Then, in 1909, the city excelled itself in 'Tragic Week'. In response to a national call-up of reserves to fight in Morocco, which *barcelonins* wanted nothing to do with, a mob took to the streets and destroyed 70 buildings of religious orders, killing 116 people and injuring 300.

Anarchy and Civil War

Catalanism was now at the centre of the political agenda and in 1914 the Mancomunitat, a local Catalan council, was established, only to be removed again in the 1923 coup by the city's military governor, Primo de Rivera, whose dictatorship lasted seven years. Elections in 1931 brought the veteran Catalan campaigner Francesc Macià to power. He declared Catalonia a republic, but it only lasted three days. Three years later his successor Lluís Companys did it again. This time Madrid sent in the army and Companys was jailed. But in 1936 the popular front was elected in Madrid and he was released. Soon afterwards, on 18 July, General Franco led the Nationalist rebellion, and the Spanish Civil War had begun.

The army in Barcelona, under General Goded, declared for Franco and marched on the city from the Bruc barracks near Pedralbes. After heavy fighting, Goded was defeated by the civil authorities and executed. Thereafter Catalonia was the staunchest of the Republican areas. But when Franco's army arrived in the city, Barcelona surrendered without a shot. Tens of thousands fled over the Pyrenees into exile, tens of thousands more were executed in reprisals. Once again the Catalan language was banned.

Above: a naval battle depicted in a painting in the Maritime Museum

The years following the Civil War were extremely hard. The rest of Europe turned its back on Madrid, and Madrid turned its back on Barcelona. But this is a region of workers who will not be kept down. The 1960s saw an economic boom and between 1960 and 1975 more than two million Spaniards came to work in the city.

A New Renaissance

On Franco's death in 1975 there was free champagne in the streets. Juan Carlos, Alfons XIII's grandson, returned to the throne and wisely some degree of autonomy was restored to Catalonia and other regions. In 1980, the conservative Jordi Pujol was elected president of Catalonia and promoted his 'country' around the world. Barcelona had embarked on another *Renaixença*, another rebirth. Schools began to teach the Catalan language again, with Castilian (Spanish) as a second language. Catalan theatre, literature and the arts were bursting with new-found energy. The 1992 Olympics gave impetus to this rebirth. Suddenly there was money to invest in the city's infrastructure, to renovate old buildings and to build new roads. This imaginative rebuilding was directed under the socialist mayor, Pasqual Maragall, a trained town planner.

After the Olympics, *barcelonins* found themselves in a new city with its axis tilted to the north. It now had a proper waterfront where the city's run-down industrial area had been cleared and the remaining warehouses in Poble Nou became fashionable for artists and designers. There was a new airport, new culture palaces such as the Museum of Contemporary Art, National Theatre, Auditorium, and more to come. In 2003 Maragall replaced Pujol as president of the Generalitat and oversaw Forum 2004, a further development of the city around the River Besós, extending the city north and adding another leisure port. Regeneration of the city centre continued, with a new rambla driven through El Raval, and the overhaul of major museums and sites. Private as well as public money has been attracted to the arts, notably from the Caixa de Catalunya savings bank.

Barcelona today is a world city with a confident air that combines its glorious past with the avant garde in a way no other does, With an enthusiasm for their city and its achievements, *barcelonins* are the first to appreciate it.

HISTORY HIGHLIGHTS

3000BC Neolithic tombs constructed beneath Carrer Montcada.

700 Iberian settlement established on Montjuïc.

Circa 230 Barcelona is founded by Hamil Barca, Carthaginian leader and father of Hannibal, whose war with Rome provokes the Romans to land in Spain, at Empúries, north of Barcelona.

200BC–AD410 Under Roman occupation Barcelona is a small town, based around Mont Tàber near the site of the cathedral. The Romans make their main base at Tarragona, to the south.

AD 412 Visigoths arrive, making Barcelona their capital from 531–48.

717 Moors occupy the city, but leave little evidence of their rule.

801 Franks, under Charlemagne, eject the Moors and set up the Spanish March, a buffer state.

878 Wilfred the Hairy (Guifré el Pilós), Count of Barcelona, consolidates the eastern Pyrenees and is given autonomy by the Franks. Thus begins 500-year family rule of the region.

1060 The Catalan constitution, called the Usatges, is drawn up.

1162 The Counts of Barcelona join a confederation with the neighbouring kingdom of Aragon, and become kings in their own right.

1213 Jaume I (The Conqueror) begins naval expansion. The Catalan Consolat de Mar establishes trading practices throughout the Mediterranean.

1395 Jocs Florals, troubadors' Olympics, are introduced. This is the period of the flowering of Catalan culture.

1479 Ferdinand of Catalonia-Aragon marries Isabella of Castile, uniting Spain.

1493 Columbus returns from the New World, but Catalonia is barred from trading with the Americas, a privilege which is given to Seville.

1640–52 Revolt of the harvesters, *els segadors*.

1714 Barcelona is sacked by Bourbon king Felipe V. The University is closed, books burned, the Catalan language banned and La Ribera district of the city is pulled down.

1808–14 The French occupy Barcelona during the Peninsula War. Montserrat is sacked.

1835 Monasteries dissolved and their properties confiscated.

1848 The first Spanish railway built between Barcelona and Mataró

1859 Revival of Jocs Florals, cornerstone of the Renaixença. Cerdà plans the rebuilding of Barcelona, in what is now the Eixample.

1888 Universal Exhibition is held in Ciutadella Park.

1901–9 Years of anarchism and strikes culminate in the Tragic Week when 70 religious institutions are razed.

1929 International Exhibition takes place in Montjuïc.

1931 Macià declares an independent Catalonia, which only lasts a few days.

1936 Spanish Civil War. The Republican government retreats from Madrid to Valencia, then to Barcelona, but is finally defeated by insurgent Nationalists led by General Franco.

1939 Franco's dictatorship begins. The Catalan language is banned from official use.

1975 Death of Franco. The Bourbon line is restored with King Juan Carlos I.

1978 Under a new constitution, semi-autonomy is granted to Catalonia. Jordi Pujol becomes first president and remains in power until 2003.

1992 Olympic Games held in Barcelona. The city is internationally recognised for its urban regeneration.

2004 Forum 2004: international cultural event based in Diagonal Mar.

Left: the fiery arrow that ignited the Olympic torch in 1992

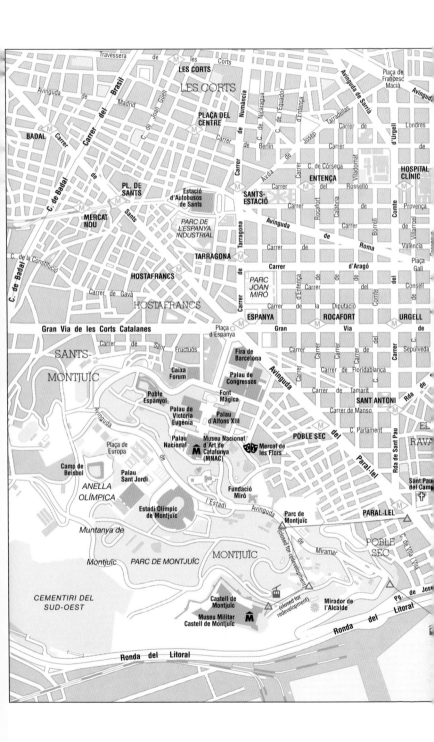

Barcelona

500 m / 550 yds

City Itineraries

B arcelona has no need of your car – it has more than enough of its own. It also has inexpensive and frequently used taxis, buses and a metro and train system that is simplicity itself: a single-fare ticket will take you to any part of the central network and beyond; a Targeta T-10 gives you 10 rides for slightly less than the price of six on trains and buses and the new trams. Transport is often a delight: cable cars and funiculars take you to the city's mountains, boat trips take you round the bay and there are even open-air escalators.

For the visitor, the city is not hard to get around and much of it can be conquered on foot. Look at the map: back from the port is the old town, the Barri Gòtic, centred on the cathedral. It has not had to suffer the modern indignity of pedestrianisation, because many of its lanes were built for nothing wider than a horse and cart in the first place. One-way signs for horse-drawn traffic are still pinned to solid stone walls.

Beside these warrens runs the famous Rambla, which leads from the old port and waterfront up to the Plaça de Catalunya, the heart of the city. From here the broad, chic shopping streets, Rambla de Catalunya and Passeig de Gràcia, run inland through the 19th-century new town, the Eixample, across the Diagonal and the Gran Via, the widest of the city's thoroughfares.

A little farther afield lie the Sagrada Família, Antoni Gaudí's great unfinished masterpiece, the Gothic monastery of Pedralbes, and the Park Güell, originally the property of Gaudí's patron, Eusebi Güell, and full of wonderfully decorative touches. There are plenty of open spaces if you need to relax, from the Parc de la Ciutadella, which also encompasses a zoo and several museums, to the Parc de Montjuïc, where the 1992 Olympic buildings were constructed. And, of course, there's Tibidabo, the summit of the Collserola hills, where there are splendid views of the city, peaceful walks, a great amusement park and the church of the Sagrat Cor.

Barcelona's port is a fascinating place to wander, and your exploration may lead you on to Barceloneta and the beaches, a once-industrial area that was regenerated for the Olympic Games and is now a great spot to eat or swim.

Dip and Delve

When the feet get tired there are always tempting cafés that need checking out. Don't be afraid to ignore your map sometimes and go slightly off the beaten track. Dive down beckoning alleys or carry on around corners which entice you with their markets, mansions or shop windows, for there is no better city in which to become lost.

Left: the towers of Gaudí's Sagrada Família
Right: Tibidabo tram

1. LA RAMBLA *(see map, p23)*

If you only have a day to spare, this is the itinerary for you. From the Plaça de Catalunya down the famous Rambla to the Boqueria market. Then dive into the Gothic quarter to see the town hall and cathedral. The Picasso museum is not far away. Return to the Rambla via the Santa Maria del Mar church and the seafront to end at the lively Plaça Reial.

Opened in 1927, the **Plaça de Catalunya** is the meeting point of the old and new cities. It is also a space for demonstrations and rock concerts. At the metro exit in the southern corner, near the statue commemorating Francesc Macià, is the **Café Zurich**, a city institution that has been rebuilt in the commercial centre, El Triangle. The world passes by its pavement tables, shoe-shiners operate, lottery tickets are sold: a good place for a coffee before starting out.

From here the famous **Rambla** begins, a 1.5-km (1-mile) long avenue of colourful bird, flower and news stands spread out beneath the shade of plane trees alongside café tables. Musicians, mime artists, tango dancers, fire eaters, fortune tellers and other entertainers ensure constant diversion at all hours of the day and night. The Rambla is in fact made up of five consecutive *rambles*: the Canaletes, Estudis, Sant Josep, Caputxins and Santa Mònica, the last three taking their names from the convents that lined the southwest (right-hand) side of the street. On the left-hand side was the medieval city's perimeter wall.

At the top of La Rambla is the cast-iron Canaletes drinking fountain, a meeting place for Barça football fans. Taste these waters, it is said, and you will come back to the city again. Further down on the right at No 115 is the **Poliorama** theatre. This was built as the Royal Academy

Above: the Rambla is the city's favourite meeting place
Left: street entertainers keep the crowds amused

of Sciences and Arts and on its facade is the city's first clock, erected in 1888 and inscribed 'Hora Official' ('Official Time').

Mare de Déu de Betlem, a renovated 17th-century baroque church, is the next notable building on the right. Opposite is the colonnade of the bookshop of the Generalitat (the Catalan autonomous government). The shop occupies part of the ground floor of the **Palau Moja**. The main entrance to the palace in Carrer Portaferrissa leads to its courtyard and temporary exhibition rooms, including the first-floor Grand Salon where there are fine baroque murals by Francesc Pla (1743–92). Another exhibition site is the nearby **Palau de la Virreina**, built by Spain's viceroy to Peru, whose young widow occupied it on its completion in 1777. It has a cultural information centre with a box office and is a good place to check out what is happening in the city.

La Boqueria, more properly the Mercat Sant Josep, is just past the mansion on the right. This is the market where the top restaurateurs do their early-morning shopping and it is a palace of food not to be passed by. Built like a great art nouveau railway station, it offers, within a few strides, all the flavours and aromas of Catalonia's countryside and cuisine. Look out for *fungi* in season, for brightly coloured vegetables and fruit, assortments of olives, cheeses and nuts, for butchers' stalls selling parts of animals you would rather not eat and, of course, seafood glistening in ice.

Beyond the market on the corner of Carrer Petxina is an attractive mosaic-fronted shop, the **Antigua Casa Figueras**, owned by the famous Barcelona chocolate makers, the Escribá family. A little further down on the left, on the corner of Carrer Cardenal Casañas, is **Casa Bruno Quadras**, an orientally inspired building with a green dragon, designed for an umbrella shop in 1891. Beyond it the road is set slightly back in the Pla de la Boqueria, which served as a place of execution during the 14th century. In the middle of the Rambla is a pavement mosaic by Joan Miró and on the far side is the city's opera house, the **Gran Teatre del Liceu** (open for visits daily 10am–1pm), rebuilt and substantially enlarged since it was destroyed in a fire in 1994.

The Barri Gòtic

It is time to leave the Rambla and dive into the Barri Gòtic, the Gothic quarter, which spreads its narrow alleys and solid walls out around the cathedral, palace and town hall. From the Pla de la Boqueria, head down the Carrer Boqueria, past Obach's hat shop into the Carrer del Call. The lane emerges into daylight at the Plaça Sant Jaume, the administrative heart of the city. The left side of the square is occupied by the elegant **Palau de la Generalitat**, from which Catalonia is governed. Opposite is the **Casa de la Ciutat**, Barcelona's town hall. It is sometimes possible to visit the town hall: enquire at the entrance, which is flanked by the figures of the saintly King Jaume I and Joan Fiveller, a 15th-century councillor who established city freedoms. The building's two most notable rooms are the 14th-century Saló del Consell de Cent, where concerts are sometimes held, and the Saló de les Cròniques where, in 1928, Josep Maria Sert painted scenes from the 14th-century Catalan expedition to Byzantium.

The Generalitat on the opposite side of the square is a Gothic building with Renaissance additions to its facade. One of the few occasions when it is

open to the public is 23 April, St George's Day. Since George (Sant Jordi) is the patron saint of Catalonia, this day calls for celebration and the square and surrounding streets are filled with stalls selling books and roses. A further reason for commemoration is that it is the anniversary of the death of Miguel de Cervantes (1547–1616) and has been declared World Book Day. The Generalitat's 15th-century St George's Chapel and first-floor Patí dels Tarongers (Orange Tree Patio, sometimes used for concerts) are among its principal architectural treasures.

The lane leading up the right-hand side of the Generalitat is the Carrer del Bisbe. On the right is the 14th-century **Casa dels Canonges** (Canons' House), now Generalitat offices. An overhead neo-Gothic bridge, based on the Bridge of Sighs in Venice, links the two buildings. Before the end of this street a portal on the right leads to the **cathedral cloisters**. Enclosed by a 15th-century iron railing, its cool atmosphere is emphasised by the mossy **Font de les Oques**, a fountain you can drink from, which takes its name from the geese which live in the cloisters.

From the cloister, enter the **Cathedral of Santa Eulàlia**, begun in 1298 under Jaume II and completed in 1417. It has three naves and a central choir. Below the altar is the crypt of Santa Eulàlia. Her remains were placed here 1,000 years after she was martyred in the Roman purges of Dacian, and her alabaster tomb, behind the altar, was carved in 1327. Of the 29 side chapels the most interesting is that of Sant Salvador, with a *Transfiguration* (1442) by Bernat Martorell. A large plaque in the baptistry on the left of the entrance says that the first six Carrib Indians brought to Europe by Columbus were baptised here on 1 April 1493.

Outside the main door is the spacious Pla de la Seu. On one side is the **Pia Almoina**, housing the Museu Diocesà, with a small but rich collection

Above: a service in the cathedral. **Above Right:** the cathedral's Gothic doorway.
Bottom Right: walkers from all walks of life

of paintings and treasures, on the other is the 15th-century **Casa de l'Ardiaca** (Archdeacon's House) built between two Roman towers, with a lovely courtyard. A letterbox decorated with swallows and a tortoise was added in 1908 by Domènech i Montaner. The street running down the opposite side of the cathedral, is the Carrer dels Comtes which leads to the **Plaça del Rei**, home of the count-kings of Catalonia-Aragon. (*To explore this area in detail, see The Royal and Roman Town, page 35.*) Exit down Carrer Veguer to **Baixada Llibreteria** or **Jaume I** to find lunch. A drink or a chocolate and *xurros* at the quaint Mesón del Café (closed Sunday) may be supplemented with pastries from nearby shops, for example a *tartaleta de music* (mixed nut tartlet) or *empanada catalana*, a pie filled with tuna and olives.

Palaces and Picasso

The **Museu Picasso** (Tues–Sun 10am–8pm; entrance fee) is 10 minutes' walk away. Continue along Baixada Llibreteria, noting the candle sellers at No 7: Pauli Subirà is the city's oldest shop and dates from 1761. Cross the busy Via Laietana and continue along the Carrer de la Princesa. The third turning on the right is **Carrer Montcada**, built by the city's aristocrats from the 12th to the 14th century. The Palau Berenguer d'Aguilar at No 15 and four neighbouring palaces house the Museu Picasso and should be visited almost as much for their splendid interiors as for the 3,000 works of art, mainly from the Spanish artist's early life.

Continue down Carrer Montcada to Passeig del Born. This area, around the old **Mercat del Born**, a 19th-century wrought-iron covered market being remodelled to show excavations of pre-18th-century houses, is becoming an increasingly fashionable artists' haunt and a popular night spot. On

the right a door leads into **Santa Maria del Mar** (9.30am–1.30pm, 4.30–8pm; entrance fee), the city's best-loved church. Built in the mid-14th century by the maritime enterprises that brought wealth and excitement to this part of town, its lofty nave reaches Catalan-Gothic heights. Pleasingly simple, its octagonal pillars are placed far apart until they close ranks around the altar to form an ambulatory. Stand by the main door to get a full sense of the space, as light from the 15th-century rose window warms even the ceiling's grey cobbles.

Exit through the main door into the Plaça Santa Maria and take the street in the far left corner, Carrer Canvis Vells, which leads to the Carrer Consolat del Mar and the **Llotja**, the former stock exchange. Picasso's father taught at the art school which occupied the upper part of the building, and Picasso and Miró were both students there. Cross back over the Via Laietana and then over the Passeig de Colom past Roy Lichtenstein's *Cap de Barcelona*.

On the Waterfront

Back on the waterfront wander along the palm-studded **Moll de la Fusta** to the **Monument a Colom** (Columbus Monument) with a lift to take you to the top for great views of the port. *(See Itinerary 8, page 44 for a guided walk around the port.)*

Cross back over to La Rambla and walk up past the Museu de la Cera (Wax Museum) on the right. The fourth turning on the left is Carrer Nou de la Rambla and just down on the left, at Nos 3–5, is **Palau Güell,** the only Gaudí building in the old town *(see El Raval, page 41).*

On the opposite side of La Rambla is the **Plaça Reial**, one of the city's liveliest squares. Cafés fill its colonnades, drug pedlars lurk on its fringes, police prowl and backpackers sleep off their overnight journeys. This is an entertaining place for *tapes* or an evening meal before strolling back up the increasingly animated Rambla to the Plaça de Catalunya.

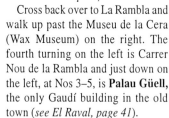

Above: looking down on Plaça Reial
Left: inside Santa Maria del Mar

2. MONTJUÏC *(see map, p28)*

Barcelona's southern hill is a place of culture, leisure and sport. This route starts at the Plaça d'Espanya, leads past the Magic Fountain, via the Mercat de les Flors and Teatre Grec, to the Fundació Miró, then leads up to the Castell de Montjuïc. The return route includes the Olympic buildings, the Museu Nacional d'Art de Catalunya and Poble Espanyol.

The buildings at the centre of the 1992 Olympic Games were the latest of many attractions in Barcelona's showground that is scattered over the 213-m (700-ft) hill of Montjuïc. Most of the grand exhibition halls and cultural palaces here are remnants of the city's last great hullabaloo, the International Exhibition of 1929.

The best way to approach Montjuïc is from the **Plaça d'Espanya**, served by Metro lines 1 and 3, outside Las Arenas, a former bullring. This allows you to walk up Avinguda de la Reina Maria Cristina through the Venetian pillars that flagged the triumphant approach to the 1929 exhibition, and past the trade fair halls towards the imposing, if not particularly beautiful, Palau Nacional. The Palau can be reached by escalators, but we will go by a more circuitous route.

At the top of the avenue is the **Font Màgica** (Magic Fountain), designed by Carles Buïgas in 1929. Rising to 50m (164ft), lit by coloured lights and accompanied by Hollywood theme tunes, it offers a grand free evening show (summer: Thur–Sun; winter: Fri–Sat). Turn left at the steps in front of the fountain where signs indicate the **Mercat de les Flors**, a complex of theatres that accommodate every possible kind of stage production.

Archaeology and Miró

Follow signs to the **Museu d'Arqueologia** in Passeig Santa Madrona (9.30am–7pm, Sun 10am–2.30pm, closed Mon; entrance fee). Built for the 1929 exhibition as the Palace of Graphic Arts, it houses finds from the city and from the Graeco-Roman trading post at Empúries on the Costa Brava. Opposite the museum is a public garden leading to the open-air **Teatre Grec**. This 1929 remnant is used for plays and concerts in the summer Grec festival.

Climb the steps at the side of the theatre to reach the **Fundació Joan Miró** (Tues–Sat 10am–7pm and Thur till 9.30pm, Sun 10am–2.30pm; entrance fee), a stunning building that is a monument to two men: the painter Joan Miró (1893–1983) and the architect Josep Lluís Sert (1902–83). They were both from Barcelona and were friends, but lived most of their lives in exile

Right: the Palau Nacional, which houses the Museu Nacional d'Art de Catalunya

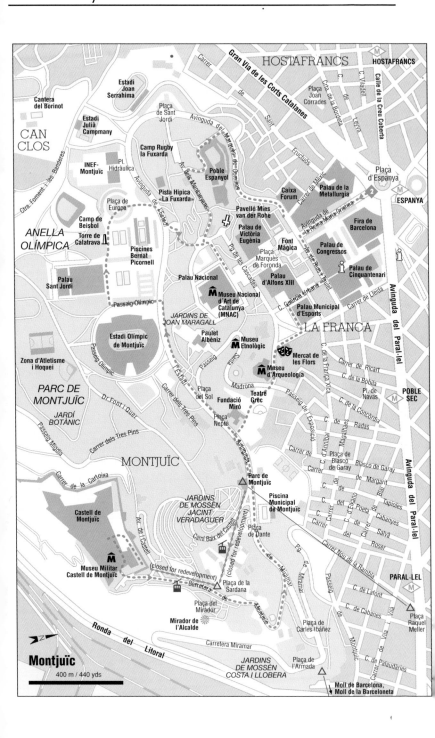

HOSTAFRANCS

Gran Via de les Corts Catalanes

Carrer

HOSTAFRANCS

Plaça Joan
Corrades

Estadi
Joan
Serrahima

Cantera
del Borinot

CAN
CLOS

Estadi
Julià
Campmany

Plaça
de Sant
Jordi

Camp Rugby
la Fuxarda

Avinguda del Marquès de Comillas

Poble
Espanyol

INEF-
Montjuïc

Pl.
Hidràulica

Pista Hípica
«La Fuxarda»

Caixa
Forum

Plaça
d'Espanya

ESPANYA

Palau de la
Metallurgia

Pavelló Mies
van der Rohe

Palau de
Victòria
Eugènia

Fira de
Barcelona

Plaça de
Europa

ANELLA
OLÍMPICA

Camp de
Beisbol

Torre de
Calatrava

Piscines
Bernal
Picornell

Font
Màgica

Plaça
Marquès
de Foronda

Palau de
Congressos

Palau de
Cinquantenari

Palau Nacional

Palau
d'Alfons XIII

Museu Nacional
d'Art de
Catalunya
(MNAC)

Palau Municipal
d'Esports

LA FRANCA

Estadi Olímpic
de Montjuïc

JARDINS DE
JOAN MARAGALL

Paulet
Albèniz

Museu
Etnològic

Mercat de
les Flors

Zona d'Atletisme
i Hoquei

Palau
Sant Jordi

Museu
d'Arqueologia

Teatre
Grec

Plaça
del Sol

Fundació
Miró

Madrona

Plaça
Neptú

PARC DE
MONTJUÏC

JARDÍ
BOTÀNIC

Dr. Font i Quer

Carrer dels Tres Pins

MONTJUÏC

Carrer de la Cartoixa

Parc de
Montjuïc

Piscina
Municipal
de Montjuïc

JARDINS
DE MOSSÈN
JACINT
VERADAGUER

Castell de
Montjuïc

Av. del Castell

Camí Baix del Castell

Plaça
de Dante

Museu Militar
Castell de Montjuïc

(closed for redevelopment)

Plaça de la
Sardana

PARAL·LEL

Plaça del
Mirador

Mirador de
l'Alcalde

Plaça de
Carles Ibáñez

Plaça
Raquel
Meller

Ronda   del   Litoral

Carretera Miramar

JARDINS
DE MOSSÈN
COSTA I LLOBERA

Plaça de
l'Armada

Montjuïc

400 m / 440 yds

Moll de Barcelona,
Moll de la Barceloneta

from the Franco regime, Miró in Paris then Mallorca, Sert at Harvard where he succeeded his mentor, Walter Gropius, as head of the faculty of architecture. Flooded with light, the gallery, which opened in 1975, houses a large collection of Miró's work, including his bright sculptures out on the roof. Concerts are held here regularly, and there's a pleasant restaurant.

View from the Top

From the gallery, continue up Avinguda de Miramar for a few minutes until the Teleferic station appears. Currently being overhauled, the cable cars will re-open in 2006. Meanwhile, a pleasant walk or bus ride will take you up to the castle. From here a new path, the Camí del Mar, skirts the hill, giving splendid views of the port as it stretches south towards the airport.

Castell de Montjuïc was built in 1640 during the Harvesters' Revolt and redesigned during the reign of Felipe V. In 1939, at the end of the civil war, it was used as a prison and execution ground. Today it houses a **Museu Militar** (Tues–Sun 9.30am–8pm; till 5pm in winter; entrance fee). Exhibits include weaponry, miniature soldiers and flags. Its battlements provide an impressive 360-degree panorama

Return down Carreterra de Montjuïc to the Plaça del Mirador. If you keep going past the Miró Foundation the buildings of the **Anella Olímpica** (Olympic Ring) will soon appear on the left. This elegant and spacious showcase includes the remodelled 1929 stadium (with a permanent exhibition of the 1992 event in the Galeria Olímpica by the south gate; Mon–Fri 10am–1pm, 4–6pm); Japanese architect Arata Isozaki's striking Palau Sant Jordi indoor sports stadium; Ricardo Bofill's neoclassical sports college; the 188-m (616-ft) Torre de Calatrava communications tower and the Plaça de Europa, from where there are some fine views over the south of the city.

Cross over Avinguda de l'Estadi to reach

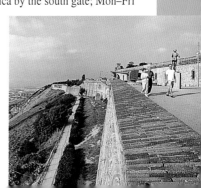

Above: the Fundació Joan Miró
Right: on the ramparts of the Castell de Montjuïc

the **Palau Nacional**, the formidable palace that dominates the approach to Montjuïc. Home to the **Museu Nacional d'Art de Catalunya** (MNAC; Tues–Sat 10am–7pm, Sun 10am–2.30pm; entrance fee), it has the finest collection of Romanesque art in the world. The most striking of its rooms are those containing wall paintings peeled off the apses of remote Pyrenean churches in the early 20th century, transported here by mule train and restored. There is a good collection of Gothic art and a smaller one of Renaissance and baroque works.

After extensive renovation work the museum now incorporates 1,000 years of Catalan art, including the 19th- and 20th-century collection from the former Museu d'Art Modern, with works by Casas, Fortuny, Mir, Nonell, Rusiñol; and the Thyssen-Bornemisza collection from Pedralbes Monastery, comprising religious paintings by Velázquez, Rubens and other masters, plus photographic and numismatic collections.

Spanish Village

Outside the Palau Nacional turn left and follow Avinguda dels Montanyans down to the **Poble Espanyol** or Spanish Village (9am till late; entrance fee includes a plan of the village). This concoction of buildings, covering 2ha (5 acres) represents architecture from all over Spain, from Moorish Andalusia to the rugged Basque country. It was designed for the 1929 exhibition and has since become a leisure centre and the 'City of Artisans' where you can see traditional glassmakers, weavers, potters and ironmngers at work and purchase their wares. Restaurants are popular in the evenings, and night spots include the Tablao del Carmen, with a flamenco show, and a trendy club, La Terraza, with open-air dancing in summer.

Turn right outside the village, and head down Avinguda del Marquès de Comillas. The **Pavelló Mies van der Rohe** (Tues–Fri 10am–8pm, Sat–Sun 11am–7pm; entrance fee) is on the right. It was built by the Bauhaus director as the German pavilion for the 1929 exhibition, later demolished, and rebuilt in 1986 to celebrate the centenary of his birth. Its glass and marble planes and unruffled pool are impressive, even after all these years.

Opposite the pavilion is a *modernista* factory, Casaramona, built in 1911 by the architect Josep Puig i Cadafalch. Now redesigned by Isozaki as the **Caixa Forum** (Tues–Sun 10am–8pm; free), it is one of the most exciting cultural spaces in the city, staging exhibitions, concerts, films and talks and with a media centre and bookshop.

Above: the Poble Espanyol has something for all age groups
Right: the entrance hall at Casa Lleó Morera

3. GAUDÍ AND THE DESIGNER CITY *(see map, p33)*

Up the Passeig de Gràcia into the Eixample to see the fine *modernista* buildings. The itinerary includes the best designer shops, a visit to the Fundació Tàpies, and ends up at the Sagrada Família and Park Güell.

Anyone who knows Barcelona will know the name of Antoni Gaudí. He made his mark on the city as Wren did on London or Eiffel on Paris. This tour of his main works takes in other examples of Modernista architecture designed by his contemporaries. It also shows the best of modern design in a city which likes to think itself stylish, and it includes the monographic museum to Barcelona's best known living artist.

Most of the city's *modernista* work is in the **Eixample** (Extension), the new part of town laid out in an 1860 grid plan by Ildefons Cerdà i Sunyer, which offered great opportunity for a newly rich bourgeoisie to build showy homes. The Rambla de Catalunya and the Passeig de Gràcia are its principle shopping streets, running from the top corners of the Plaça de Catalunya.

Start at the Passeig de Gràcia Metro, on lines 2, 3 and 4. Unmissable on the western side, between Carrer d'Aragó and Carrer del Consell de Cent at Nos 35–43, is a trilogy of Catalan *modernista* works. On the southern corner of the block is the **Casa Lleó Morera**, privately owned and closed to the public. Three houses further on is **Casa Amatller**, with an information centre for the Ruta del Modernisme. Next to it is Gaudí's **Casa Batlló**, the facade covered in blue-green ceramic work, and the windows sensuously curved. It is now open to the public (daily 9am–8pm; entrance fee).

These three buildings are known as the 'Illa de la Discordia', the Island of Discord, and each of them is striking in different ways. The architect of Casa Lleó Morera was Lluís Domènech i Montaner (1850–1923: for his masterpiece, the Palau de la Música Catalana, *see Itinerary 6, page 40*). He was the mentor of Josep Puig i Cadafalch (1867–1957), designer of the neighbouring Dutch-gabled Casa Amatller. Both were polymaths, parliamentarians, literary luminaries and leading figures of the Renaixença, the Catalan Renaissance begun in the 19th century.

Antoni Gaudí i Cornet (1852–1926), by contrast, was a single-minded

architect, and though as fiercely Catalan as the others he was a private person, a reactionary with deep religious convictions who became a recluse in later life. At the age of 74 he was run down by a tram and, mistaken for a tramp, he was taken to the old hospital in El Raval where he died two days later.

After the Island of Discord, turn left into Carrer d'Aragó. At No 255, on the north side, crowned with a twisted metal sculpture called 'Cloud and Chair', is the **Fundació Tàpies** (Tues–Sun 10am–8pm; entrance fee). It houses a large collection of Tàpies' own work and regularly holds visiting exhibitions.

Antoni Tàpies, born in Barcelona in 1923, was a friend of Miró and became identified with a separate Catalan culture through his work, which is abstract and uncompromising. The foundation is part gallery and part study centre, with a handsome library. Designed by Lluís Domènech i Montaner as an office for his brother's publishing company, it was built in 1880 and was the first domestic construction in the city to employ an iron frame.

From La Pedrera to the Sagrada Família

Return down Aragó to the wide, tree-lined Passeig de Gràcia, cross the road and walk up to No 92 on the corner of Carrer de Provença, where Casa Milà, often called **La Pedrera** is situated. Its name means the Stone Quarry, and was inspired by its rippling grey stone facade. This is Gaudí's most prominent private building, an eight-storey apartment block devoid of straight lines, set around two inner courtyards. Gaudí put the city's first underground carriage park in the basement and sculpted a roof of evil-looking chimneys that have gained the name *espantabruixes*, witch-scarers. Begun in 1901, this was an extremely controversial project. After years of being allowed to fall into decay it was rescued when UNESCO declared it of world interest and the Caixa de Catalunya undertook its restoration. The courtyard, lofts, a show flat and rooftop can be visited (daily 10am–8pm; entrance fee).

Just beyond La Pedrera, at No 96, is **Vinçon**, the leading designer store for household goods, from stylish stationery to furniture and fabrics, and there are often exhibitions. Go upstairs to appreciate the building fully. This was once the home of the artist Ramón Casas (1866–1932).

At Plaça Rei Joan Carles I, turn down Avinguda Diagonal. On the right, at No 373, is the **Palau Baró de Quadras** by Puig i Cadafalch (1904), now housing Casa Asia, an Oriental culture centre well worth visiting. There is a beautiful small courtyard, lovely glass balconies on the second floor, a cafe

Above: the spooky chimneys of La Pedrera, with the Sagrada Família in the background

and rooftop terrace. Puig i Cadafalch's **Casa de les Punxes** (House of the Spikes), officially called Casa Terrades, is a neo-Gothic apartment building on the opposite side of the avenue two blocks further down. You can't go inside, but the exterior, with three handsome doorways, is impressive.

Turn right down Carrer de Roger de Llúria and at the corner of Carrer de Mallorca are the **Palau Casades** on the north side (now inhabited by the Il.lustre Col.legi d'Advocats) and on the south side **Palau Montaner** with attractive tiled eaves. It was designed by Domènech i Montaner, again for his brother but this time as a private home and the whole family lived here from 1893 until 1939. It is now a government building.

Domènech i Montaner also built **Casa Thomas** at Carrer de Mallorca 291–3, a few yards down on the left. This is occupied by **b.d. Ediciones de Diseño**, the city's most prestigious design organisation (Mon–Sat 10am–2pm, 4–8pm). Its products are top quality, from beautiful Fortuny lampshades and Gaudí furniture to the best in modern work by local designers such as Oscar Tusquets, and others from a number of different countries. The showrooms are set out on two floors with a further room at the back.

After Gaudí had completed his last commission – Casa Milà – in 1910, he devoted the remaining 16 years of his life to the Expiatory Temple of the Holy Family, the **Sagrada Família** (Apr–Sept: daily 9am–8pm; Oct–Mar: 9am–6pm; entrance fee; guided tours available; combined ticket option to Park Güell). To reach the building, which is 10 minutes' walk from b.d., continue along Carrer de Mallorca and cross the Diagonal by the monument to the Catalan poet-priest, Jacinct Verdaguer. As you do so, you will see in the street running north the **Casa Macaya**, which was designed by Puig i Cadafalch and is currently used by the prestigious La Caixa Foundation. Peep inside to see the graceful arches of the patio and the decorated staircase.

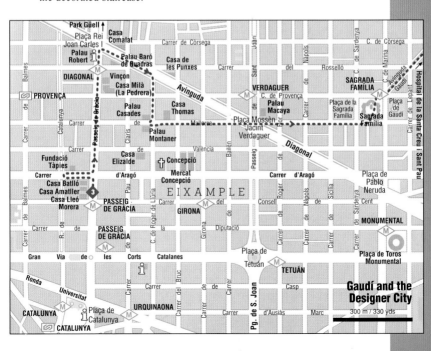

Gaudí and the Designer City

300 m / 330 yds

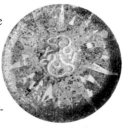

The street approaches the Sagrada Família from the west front, with statues by a local sculptor, Josep Maria Subirachs, and a Japanese one, Etsuro Soto. The only facade Gaudí completed is the eastern one dedicated to the Nativity, with three doorways to Faith, Hope and Charity, and four coloured, tentacled towers, one of which has an internal lift to take vertigo-free visitors skywards.

The crypt where Gaudí is buried also houses the museum which shows how he envisaged the finished temple, and also shows that his ideas often changed. A scale model reveals how the pillars in the nave, which has served as a builder's yard, will be like an avenue of trees in an enchanted wood.

At 110m (360ft) in length, the Sagrada Família will eventually be 27m (87ft) longer than the city's cathedral and nearly twice the height, with a main tower rising to 198m (650ft), half as high again as those that are already there. Gaudí spent his last 10 dedicated and unpaid years in a hut on the site. He didn't have much time for his own comforts, but a glimpse of his own surroundings can be had in the house where he lived in Park Güell.

Park Güell

There are several ways of reaching **Park Güell**: hop on the Tourist Bus outside the Sagrada Família; take the Metro to Lesseps, then walk 1,200 metres (½ mile) or take the No 24 bus; or walk from the Sagrada Família up the Avinguda Gaudí to Domenech i Montaner's spectacular **Hospital de la Santa Creu i Sant Pau** (still functioning, but worth a visit) from where the No 92 bus goes for Park Güell. Or hail a cab.

The entrance to the park is flanked by two pavilions designed by Gaudí. The one on the left is a shop. The one on the right has an exhibition that gives a background to the building of the park, which is always popular. Children play around its coloured animals and chase between the pillars that support the wavy, tile-mosaic parapet from where there is a grand view out over the city. This long, curving bench, perhaps most photographed aspect of the park,

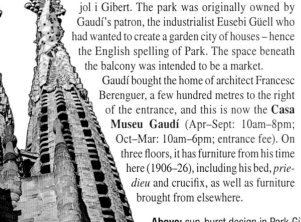

was the work not of Gaudí but of his assistant, Josep Jujol i Gibert. The park was originally owned by Gaudí's patron, the industrialist Eusebi Güell who had wanted to create a garden city of houses – hence the English spelling of Park. The space beneath the balcony was intended to be a market.

Gaudí bought the home of architect Francesc Berenguer, a few hundred metres to the right of the entrance, and this is now the **Casa Museu Gaudí** (Apr–Sept: 10am–8pm; Oct–Mar: 10am–6pm; entrance fee). On three floors, it has furniture from his time here (1906–26), including his bed, *prie-dieu* and crucifix, as well as furniture brought from elsewhere.

Above: sun-burst design in Park Güell
Left: the spires remain unfinished

4. THE ROYAL AND ROMAN TOWN *(see map, p36)*

This tour takes a more detailed look at the historic and royal Barri Gòtic quarter, starting at the Plaça Nova.

The **Plaça Nova** is at the west end of Avinguda Catedral, the large open space in front of the cathedral (Metro to Liceu, Line 3, or Jaume I, Line 4). From here the Roman wall that encircled the 4th-century city begins its surviving 1.5-km (1-mile) stretch. It is easily identified by its colossal stones, the largest of which is 3.5m (12ft) thick and 9.5m (30ft) high. The Roman city wall had 78 towers and two remain in Plaça Nova, marking the **Portal del Bisbe**, the north gate. These are incorporated into the **Casa de l'Ardiaca** (Archdeacon's House, *see page 25*). On the far side of the cathedral square the wall continues past the 15th-century almshouse, Pia Almoina, running down Carrer de la Tapineria to Plaça Ramón Berenguer el Gran. The equestrian statue here of the 12th-century count, who added Provence in France to Catalonia by marriage, is by Josep Llimona (1864–1934).

   Behind him the royal palace complex of the count-kings of Barcelona-Aragon grew from the Roman wall incorporating a Roman watchtower for the bell tower of its chapel. To reach it, continue down Tapineria, turn right into Carrer Llibreteria, right again into Carrer Veguer and into the **Plaça del Rei**. This imposing square of solid doorways and tawny towers, redolent of counts and courtiers, is the city's Gothic heart.

The Royal Palace

The palace complex is visited via the **Museu d'Història de la Ciutat** (City History Museum; Oct–May: Tues–Sun 10am–2pm, 4–8pm, Sun 10am–3pm; Jun–Sept: 10am–8pm; entrance fee includes admission to the Royal Palace and Chapel). The museum occupies the 17th-century Casa Clariana-Padellàs, a merchant's house brought here, stone by stone, in 1930. In the process of re-erecting it, Roman remains were excavated and now a large section of foundations of the Roman town have been opened up beneath here and the royal palace on the far side of the square. These subterranean rooms show streets of shops and industries, from textile dyeing to wine making. They also chart the development of the first Christian palace that prefigured the palace of the Barcelona count-kings.

   Emerging from this Roman twilight, the visitor arrives in the **Palau Reial Major**, a building mostly taken up by the **Saló del Tinell**, the Royal Palace's great hall and throne room. Its enormous interior stone arches were designed in the 14th century for Pere III (the Ceremonious) by Guillem Carbonell, who was also responsible for much of the palace's facade. Columbus

Right: the tawny towers of the Plaça del Rei

is said to have been received in the Tinell by Ferdinand and Isabella and this is where the Inquisition held its courts. Today it is a venue for concerts and exhibitions. The Royal Chapel of **Santa Agata**, built for Jaume II (the Just) in 1312, contains the only adornment in the complex. Jaume's coat of arms can be seen behind the fine retable of the Epiphany painted by Jaume Huguet in 1446, while scenes of poor Agatha's martyrdom are depicted in a chapel on the left.

A narrow flight of steps behind a door on the right of the nave leads up past the Saló del Tinell into the distinctive, five-storey **Watchtower of Marti I**, the Humanist (1396–1410), who was the last of the 500-year dynasty of Catalan counts. The tower domi-

nates the Plaça del Rei where the only remaining building is the **Palau del Lloctinent**, which, when remodelled, will complete the royal buildings in this harmonious square. The Lloctinent, or lord lieutenant, was the viceroy of Carlos V. The post was created in the late 18th century but the palace was built between 1549 and 1557 by Antoni Carbonell, and though it has such classic Catalan Gothic touches as the plain fan-stone portal, it is a Renaissance building with a splendid courtyard. It is used to contain the Archives of the Crown of Aragon, which include monastic documents going back to the 9th century.

Above: historical costumes on display in the Museu Frederic Marès

Religious Artefacts

One further place in this royal complex needs to be visited, and that is the **Museu Frederic Marès** (Tues–Thur 10am–5pm, Wed, Fri–Sat 10am–6pm, Sun 10am–3pm; entrance fee). It lies directly behind the Tinell in what were the palace gardens; its entrance is a few metres beyond the Palau del Lloctinent's other entrance in the Carrer dels Comtes. This building started life in the 13th century as the bishop's palace, then became home to the counts of Barcelona and the count-kings of Barcelona-Aragon.

It now houses an extraordinary collection of mainly religious artefacts brought together by Marès, a wealthy local sculptor who had an apartment in the building and lived there until his death, at the age of 97, in 1991. There is a large Romanesque collection, particularly crucifixes, as well as entire portals. On the upper floors is a delightful hotchpotch of memorabilia from all ages of toys, pipes, locks, lacework, clocks, cameras and even pin-up postcards, and Marès's own study and studio.

5. THE JEWISH QUARTER *(see pull-out map)*

The narrow streets between La Rambla and the Cathedral, north of Carrer Ferran, still bear some traces of the city's medieval Jewish population, expelled 600 years ago.

As in many parts of the old city, the pleasure here is simply in walking the streets, peering into patios, window shopping, menu reading and wondering at the history heaped up behind walls of solid stone. Enter the Carrer Boqueria from La Rambla (Metro Line 3 to Liceu) and continue up the **Carrer del Call**, a lane of jewellers' shops. A Jewish quarter is a *call* in Catalan (the word comes from the Hebrew *qahqal*, meaning 'meeting'), and this is where a substantial population of the Jews lived from the 12th century. They were cultured teachers and prosperous merchants and they built the first university in Catalonia. In the 14th century, a build-up of anti-semitism led to the walling off of the *call* into a ghetto, with the only entrance at the end of Carrer del Call in Plaça Sant Jaume. In 1391, following widescale rioting in the wake of accusations that the Jews had brought the Black Death to Spain, the *call* was virtually destroyed, many of its residents murdered, and the rest given the choice of conversion or expulsion. A century later all non-Catholic religions were banned altogether.

From Carrer del Call turn up Sant Domènec del Call where some houses date back to the 12th century. A synagogue is thought to have been on the site of No 7, and a secondary syn-

Right: a street in the Jewish Quarter

agogue was built at the end of the street in 1379. Both sites are now private houses. In the parallel Carrer Arc de Sant Ramon the Sinagogo de los Franceses was built in 1506. The streets are connected by two lanes, Carrer Fruita and Carrer Marlet. In the wall of No 1 Carrer Marlet is a **Hebrew memorial stone** dated 1314 which reads simply: 'Holy foundation of Rabbi Samuel Hassardi for whom life never ends. Year 62'. At No. 5 is the newly revealed **Sinagoga Major** (11am–2.30pm, 4–7.30pm), which shows a part of what is thought to have been the largest synagogue in the city before the property passed to the monarchy after the uprising in 1391.

At the top of Carrer Sant Domènec del Call are Carrer Sant Sever and Baixada Santa Eulàlia, a continuous, sloping alley where furniture restorers work in sunless, cavernous basements. From Carrer Sant Sever there is access into the shady Plaça Sant Felip Neri where the **Museu del Calçat** (Museum of the History of Footwear; Tues–Sun 11am–2pm; entrance fee) displays the largest shoe in the world, made to fit the statue of Christopher Columbus at the bottom of La Rambla, and a gold stiletto-heeled shoe worn by the opera singer, Victoria de los Angeles.

Characterful Quarter

Turn back down Sant Domènec del Call and cross the Plaça Manuel Ribé to Carrer Arc Sant Ramón del Call, right into Carrer del Call and right again at the Obach hat shop into **Carrer Banys Nous**, the 'Street of the New Baths'. There were baths here until the early 19th century. This is one of the most characteristic streets of the old quarter, and among its commercial premises are a quaint dairy and one of the last of Barcelona's great *bodegas*, the **Portalón**. At the top of this street turn left into Carrer de la Palla, which leads into **Plaça Sant Josep Oriol**. This delightful square has a weekend art market, and the adjoining **Plaça del Pi** has a local food produce market from Friday to Sunday on the first and third weeks of the month. Beside them rise the 14th-century **Santa Maria del Pi**, distinguished by its stained-glass windows.

Before settling for a drink in the square, a final detour should be made up **Carrer Petritxol** in the northwest corner of Plaça del Pi. This is an attractive street of art galleries and chocolate shops. Sala Parés at No 5 dates from 1845, and was the first gallery to exhibit Picasso's work.

Above: an ornate facade in the Plaça del Pi
Right: the auditorium of the Palau de la Música Catalana

6. SECRETS OF THE OLD TOWN *(see map, p40)*

A less-trodden route through the Old Town, taking in historical highlights from Roman days to Modernisme, strolling through today's busy streets and ending in the latest and most indulgent of Barcelona's 80 museums, the Museu de la Xocolata.

Begin in Plaça Catalunya, at its best in the early morning light, and follow the short road beside the Hard Rock Café into the hidden square of Plaça Ramón Amadeu. At its far end the two-tiered Gothic cloisters of the medieval church of **Santa Anna** (Mon–Sat 9am–1pm, 6.30–8pm) are a haven from the surrounding commercial din. Built for the Knights Templars in the 12th century, its cloister and chapter house remain standing. From the bustling street of Santa Anna go down Bertrellans, opposite the wonderful fan shop *Guantería Alonso*, into **Plaça de la Vila de Madrid**. With luck the dazzling jacaranda will be in flower in this quiet square, which has a Roman necropolis, discovered in the 1950s. The square has been landscaped recently to show off its Roman treasure, and a restaurant has opened in the Ateneu, a traditional Catalan cultural organisation on the corner. Opposite you will find Decathlon, a popular sports emporium where bikes can be hired.

Follow Passatge Duc de la Victòria and go back up to Canuda and into Portal de l'Angel. A busy shopping area, ideal if you're hunting for shoes or moderately priced fashion, but best avoided on Saturday. Cut diagonally across it into Montsió, where a *modernista* building is tucked away. Designed in 1897 by Puig i Cadafalch, **Casa Martí** became the famous café **Els Quatre Gats** (Four Cats), frequented by Barcelona's artistic circle at the turn of the century, and where the 19-year-old Picasso had his first exhibition in 1900. You can try to catch the fervent atmosphere of the time by having the reasonably priced lunch *menú*, but it may be better to have a quick drink, absorb the decorative details and wander round the corner to a more genuine bar where the locals eat, like Mercé de Vins in Carrer Amargós. This pretty

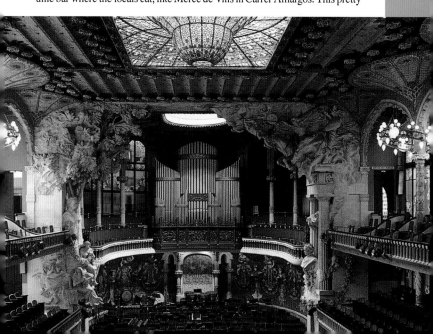

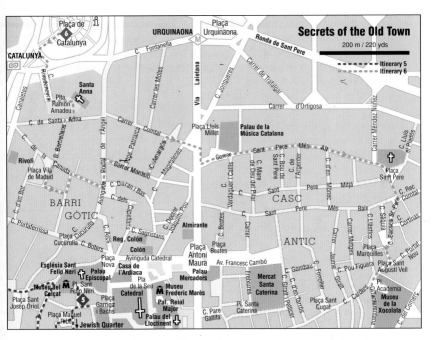

street takes pride in itself; ceramic plaques proclaim it 'the first street in Barcelona to have paraffin lights' and the shops are unusual and attractive.

Silk, Music and Chocolate

Turn right at the end of Carrer Amargós into Carrer Comtal and cross over busy, dusty Via Laietana into Sant Pere Més Alt, noticing at No 1 the fine example of *esgrafiat* (decorative relief work on the facade). This is the Casal de Gremi de Velers (the Silk Industry Guild), marking the beginning of a *barri* still dedicated to the textile industry. A visit to the **Palau de la Música Catalana** is essential, either on a guided tour (daily 10.30am–3pm, later in summer; booking advisable) or by attending a concert. This extravaganza of *modernista* architecture, built in 1908 by Domènech i Montaner and now a UNESCO World Heritage Site, is a bold, colourful building of tiles, mosaics and statuary with wonderful stained glass that suffuses the intimate auditorium with mellow light. The acoustics aren't bad, either. Its recent extension by Oscar Tusquets includes a chamber concert hall and a gourmet restaurant.

The network of streets beyond, between Sant Pere Més Alt (Upper) and Sant Pere Més Baix (Lower), full of tiny drapers shops, is worth exploring. From **Plaça Sant Pere**, with an ancient church and Modernista fountain, take Basses Sant Pere to Plaça Sant Agustí Vell then Tantarantana to the final treat, the **Museu de la Xocolata** (Comerç 36; Mon–Sat 10am–8pm, Sun till 3pm) in the old convent of Sant Agustí. Here you can follow the story of chocolate, discovered by Spain and brought to Europe, and see imaginative chocolate statuary. In its *xocolateria* you can taste an authentic cup of hot chocolate.

7. EL RAVAL *(see map, p42)*

El Raval is the part of the old town on the opposite side of La Rambla to the Barri Gòtic, bounded by the Ronda de Sant Pau and the Avinguda Paral.lel. This tour takes in the city's oldest church and hospital as well as the ultra-modern Museu d'Art Contemporani de Barcelona (MACBA).

Neglected for years and ill-famed for drugs, delinquency and prostitution, this district, once the notorious Barri Xinès (or Barrio Chino), is undergoing a metamorphosis, using drastic measures and municipal funding. Trendy bars, shops and art galleries now mingle with what remains of 'local colour'.

Head into El Raval down Carrer Nou de la Rambla, between the Liceu and Drasssanes metro stops on the Rambla. On the left is **Palau Güell** (temporarily closed for refurbishment). Designed by Gaudí for Count Eusebi Güell for his town house, it has a rather gloomy atmosphere but is fascinating nevertheless, with an extraordinary roof and chimneys that Güell never visited. He only lived in the house for a couple of years.

Continue down this street of small shops and at the end turn up into Carrer Abat Safont around the back of **Sant Pau del Camp**, at the western end of the Carrer de Sant Pau. This is Barcelona's oldest church, first Roman, then Visigothic and rededicated after the Moorish incursions of 1117. The lintel and marble capitals on the west portal are from the 7th century. The **monastery** is approached through a door to the right, which leads to a small, attractive cloister with cinquefoil and trefoil arches (Mon–Sat 10am–1pm, 5–8pm, Sun 10am–4pm). A gravestone, used first for a Roman, bears an inscription to Guifre (Wilfred) II Borrell who in 897 became the second ruler of the Barcelona dynasty. He is the probable benefactor of the monastery.

Carry on up Carrer Sant Pau until the new **Rambla del Raval** opens up. This thoroughfare was only recently bulldozed through the heart of the Barri Xinès, and it is lively day and night with an industrious immigrant population.

To Market

At the top of the street turn left along the streets Hospital and Sant Antoni Abat to the **Mercat de Sant Antoni**, one of the city's large, attractive iron halls (1882). During the week this serves as a food market, with clothes and haberdashers' stalls behind the encircling green blinds, and on Sunday morning (10am–2pm) there are second-hand book and video stalls to browse through .

Take the same route back into El Raval from the market. This is a fascinating street of herbalists, pharmacists

Right: the magnificent Romanesque doorway of Sant Pau del Camp

and Arab pastry shops. On the left is a pedestrian street, Riera Baixa, full of second-hand clothes shops.

The 16th-century facade of the **Antic Hospital de la Santa Creu** soon looms up on the left and, just beyond it, La Capella, its small 15th-century church, now an exhibition space. Through the main archway lie the former hospital grounds where people come to sit quietly, much as convalescing patients must have done for 500 years. The convalescent house was set up in the 15th century and remained the city's

principle hospital until Santa Creu i Sant Pau was built in 1910 near the Sagrada Família *(see page 33)*. The hospital buildings are now devoted to the Massana Art School, Institute of Catalan Studies and the Library of Catalonia. Walk through to the second square and on the left you will see an entrance into the **Convalescence House Gardens**, richly decorated with coloured tiles by Llorens Passolles in 1681.

Modern Art

Leave the hospital by turning left down Carrer del Carme and then right into Carrer dels Angels through the Plaça Angels to the ice-white **Museu d'Art Contemporani de Barcelona** (MACBA; winter: Mon, Wed–Fri 11am–7.30pm; summer: 10am–8pm; Sat 10am–8pm, Sun 10am–3pm all year; entrance fee) designed by American architect Richard Meier. It's a brilliant space on three floors showing post-war Catalan and Spanish art, and temporary exhibitions.

Beside it, in the old Casa de Caritat (once a poorhouse and orphanage), is the magnificent **Centre de Cultura Contemporània** (CCCB; winter: Tues, Thur, Fri 11am–2pm, 4–8pm; Wed, Sat 11am–8pm; Sun 11am–7pm; summer: Tues–Sat 11am–8pm, Sun 11am–3pm; entrance fee), offering a programme of exhibitions, concerts, dance and films.

Left: one of El Raval's trendy second-hand shops
Right: the *Amérigo Vespucci* in the harbour

8. PORT VELL *(see map, p44)*

From the Drassanes Museu Marítim to Barceloneta, around the city's leisurely old port.

Port Vell, the old port of Barcelona, is a focal point of leisure pursuits centred on the Moll d'Espanya where the Maremàgnum shopping, restaurant and cinema complex, L'Aquàrium and Imax cinema have added glamour to the old yachting basin. Vessels from the city's two yacht clubs have to wait for the swing bridge to open on the pedestrian Rambla de Mar, to let them out into the sea. As with any port there is always activity, among the gin palaces and visiting tall ships in the Marina Esportiva, the cruise liners on the Moll de Barcelona, the trawlers in Barceloneta and the pleasure boats that conduct trips round the port.

The Old Shipyards

The port's nearest Metro stop is Drassanes at the bottom of the Rambla (Line 3). This is the name of the city's former shipyards, which have been refurbished as a museum, the **Museu Marítim** (10am–7pm; entrance fee includes audio guides), a good place to begin a tour of maritime Barcelona. Situated beyond the end of La Rambla, on the right, the revitalised shipyards are enclosed by the city's 15th-century outer wall, which stretches round into Avinguda del Paral.lel where the Portal de Santa Madrona tower and gateway also remain.

The Drassanes is the place that launched a thousand ships, a soaring cathedral of *naves*. The sheds, put up in 1378 and greatly enlarged in the 17th century, were the first arsenal in Spain, preceded in the Mediterranean only by Venice. At their height they were turning out 30 war galleys at a time, which they were hastily doing as the Christian west prepared for a final showdown with the Muslim Ottomans in 1571 at Lepanto off the Greek coast. A full-scale replica of Don John's victorious flagship, the *Reial*, is the centrepiece of the museum. This great golden galley, with banks of oars to drive it head-on into its foe, bore the *Lepanto Christ*, a crucifix now in Barcelona cathedral. The museum, which spreads throughout the large, impressive halls, charts Catalonia's sea-faring history with a collection of fishing boats and model naval ships, with a model-making workshop, plus

reconstructions of wharves, rope-makers' lofts, cabins, agents' offices and artefacts that all add up to a full account of the city's maritime past. There is a cafe, shop and good restaurant.

The nearby **Monument a Colom**, the Columbus Monument, is a traffic island, and the reward for patiently waiting to cross to it is a ride up the internal lift to a viewing platform at the top of this 60-m (200-ft) column, open most daylight hours. It was designed by Gaietà Buïgas, with a crowning sculpture of the Genoan navigator by Rafael Arché, for the Universal Exhibition of 1888. It stands in the Plaça Portal de la Pau (Gate of Peace Square) through which Christopher Columbus, his wife, three sons, seven Carib Indians and fellow explorers entered the city on his return from the West Indies in April 1493.

In front of the statue is the waterfront Moll de les Drassanes where the *golondrina* (swallow) pleasure boats offer trips to the entrance of the harbour or to the Olympic port. To the left is the **Junta d'Obres del Port**, the Port Authority building constructed in 1907 as a reception point for passengers.

Go over the wooden Rambla de Mar to the Moll d'Espanya, the main jetty of Port Vell. The cinema and shopping complex of **Maremàgnum**, with plenty of places for refreshment, leads to **L'Aquarium** (summer: daily 9.30am–10pm; winter: daily 10am–9pm; entrance fee). This underwater world shows what snorkel divers are likely to see in the surrounding seas, and an imaginative tunnel leads visitors among sharks and rays.

Beyond the Junta d'Obres on the shore is the old timber wharf, the **Moll de la Fusta**, redesigned as a palm-lined promenade in the late 1980s by Manuel de Solà-Morales. It leads to the Moll d'Espanya and the **Marina Esportiva** where the mega-rich tie up their yachts. In former times this was

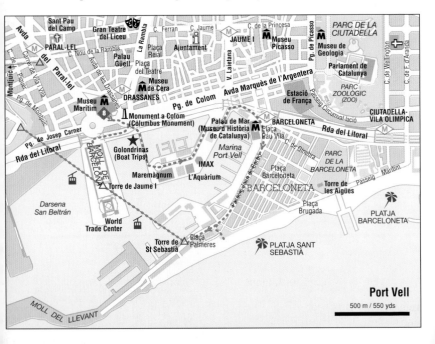

a dock area with bustling warehouses. The only one left is Elies Rogent's 1878 brick-built Magatzem General, now the **Palau del Mar**. Dockside restaurants are based here, and part of the building is the excellent **Museu d'Història de Catalunya** (Tues, Thur–Sat 10am–7pm; Wed 10am-8pm; Sun 10am–2.30pm; entrance fee). It covers two substantial floors, the first of which takes one up to the 18th century, the second begins with industrialisation and includes intruguing memories of the Franco years.

Cable Car Ride
To complete the round trip of Port Vell, you could stroll down to the **Torre de Sant Sebastià** cable car. A lift ascends the iron hulk of a tower to a platform where the enclosed buckets of the **Aeri del Port** fly over the harbour towards the **World Trade Center** and the cruise ship terminal on the Moll de Barcelona. You could get off here and head back to the Columbus Monument; alternatively, wander through Barceloneta's streets to reach the city's closest beaches *(see Itinerary 13, page 52)*.

9. CIUTADELLA PARK *(see pull-out map)*

Within this peaceful park's boundaries are several museums and cultural centres, the Catalan parliament and the zoo.

The 34-ha (75-acre) **Parc de la Ciutadella** is a large breathing space beside the old city, and its zoological and geological museums and zoo make it a good place for children. Its many varieties of trees are well labelled, and the palms attract squawking parrots escaped from their cages on La Rambla. The park takes its name from a star-shaped citadel built by Felipe V after besieging the city in 1714. After the fortress was torn down the park was laid out, in 1873, by Josep Fontseré. The Ciutadella-Vila Olímpica Metro (Line 4) is on its south side in the Olympic Village, but only has access to the park via the zoo.

A better option is **Arc de Triomf** (Line 1) on the north side, at the end of Passeig de Lluís Companys where the city's law courts are. The station is named after an arch that echoes the one in Paris. It was designed by Josep Vilaseca i Casanovas as the entrance to the Universal Exhibition of 1888.

On the north side of the park are Fontseré's fountains and grottos, and just beyond a pleasant boating lake with a variety of ducks.

Most of the exhibition buildings were hastily erected and not meant to last, with the notable exception of Lluís Domènech i Montaner's **Café-Restaurant**. This

Left: the Columbus Monument
Right: a detail on the Arc de Triomf

castle-like building, modelled on the Llotja (Stock Exchange) in Valencia, was an arts and crafts centre for a while afterwards and set the young architects of Barcelona on the path towards Modernisme. Today a visitor may be forgiven for thinking this crenellated red-brick fort, more often known as the **Castell del Tres Dragons** (Castle of the Three Dragons), is the citadel after which the park is named. Impossible to miss, it is on the edge of the park beside the Passeig de Picasso. A parliament assembled here in 1917. In 1934, it became the **Museu de Zoologia**, the Zoological Museum (Tues–Sun 10am–2pm; entrance fee), which has a Victorian collection of stuffed animals.

To the south is the **Museu de Geologia** (Tues–Sun 10am–2pm; entrance fee), bright with crystals, minerals and fossils, in a neoclassical building.

On either side of the museum lie the greenhouses of the **Hivernacle**, an idyllic setting for jazz concerts in summer, and Fontseré's **Umbracle**, a palm house. Just outside in Passeig de Picasso is the glass cube entitled *Homenatje a Picasso,* by Antoni Tàpies.

Five minutes' walk away is the centre of the park and the **Plaça d'Armes** where *Sorrow*, by Josep Llimona, crouches in the central pond. The buildings each side of it are all that remain of the citadel built by the victorious Bourbon king, Felipe V. They were used as a prison, captured by Napoleon, demolished, rebuilt, handed back to the town and bombed in the civil war. On the west side is a small chapel and beside it is the former local governor's palace of 1748, now a school.

Government and Animals

On the opposite, eastern, side of the square is the former arsenal, which was made a royal palace when the park became a leisure ground in the late 19th century. Today it is occupied by the **Catalan parliament.** The Museu d'Art Modern de Catalunya was also here until 2004 when its collection was absorbed into the Museu Nacional d'Art de Catalunya on Montjüic(*see page 30).*

The entrance to the **Zoo** (May–Aug: daily 9.30am–7.30pm; Sept–Apr: 10am–5pm; entrance fee) is by the southern gate. There are elephants, hippos, big cats and performing dolphins. The most famous inmate was the late lamented Snowflake (Floc de Neu), the only albino gorilla in captivity.

In front of the zoo there is a fountain with a sculpture of a young woman holding an umbrella that keeps the water from her elegant clothes. *La Dama del Paraigues* by Roig i Soler is a kind of mascot of the city.

Above: there are regular dolphin shows at the Barcelona Zoo

10. ¡BARÇA! *(see map, p48)*

A visit to Barcelona's football stadium and museum.

After the Picasso Museum, the Barcelona football club museum is the most visited in the city. Fans from all over the world come to see Europe's largest stadium, to wonder at the trophies, watch the playbacks, gloat over past glories and stand in the directors' box. The stadium, called **Camp Nou** (New Field), has been extended since it was built in 1957 and can now hold some 100,000. It is the largest constituent part of a sports complex just below the university campus and the smart end of Avinguda Diagonal. Basketball, hockey, handball, junior football and ice hockey are also catered for in its neighbouring buildings, the **Mini Estadi**, the **Palau Blaugrana** (*blau* translates as blue, *grana* as burgundy: the club colours) and the **Pista de Gel** ice rink.

Ticket First

Take Metro Line 5 to Collblanc. Turn immediately up Francesc Layret and right into Travessera de les Corts, then second left beside the perimeter fence up Carrer d'Arístides Maillol. The main ticket office is on this corner and tickets are on sale week days 9am–1pm, 4–8pm. Same-day tickets can be bought in ticket offices on Avinguda Les Corts or Avinguda Joan XXIII. Match times vary between 5 and 9pm (usually on Sunday) according to the time of year. *Entrada general* are the cheapest tickets for the top tier of the stadium. *Lateral* are good, middle-priced seats and *Tribuna* are the covered, more expensive seats.

Continue up Arístides Maillol and follow the signs to the **museum** (Mon–Sat 10am–6.30pm; Sun 10am–2pm; entrance fee includes 45-minute tour of dressing rooms, tunnel to pitch, players' benches, presidential box and press room). This is one of the world's richest football clubs and about 100,000 members have permanent seats in the stunning ground. There is no shortage of souvenirs in the two-storey **FC Botiga Megastore**.

Return the way you came; if you want to visit the Pedralbes Palace and Monastery just north of here, *see Itinerary 11, page 48.*

Above: a floodlit match at Camp Nou

11. PEDRALBES PALACE
AND MONASTERY *(see map below)*

A route that also includes the ceramic and decorative arts museum in the royal palace, a peaceful medieval monastery and a glimpse of the Güell estate.

Pedralbes monastery is the finest surviving Gothic building in the city. Set in one of the wealthiest districts, it nevertheless has a pleasant, away-from-it-all feeling. In winter, make an early start – the monastery closes at 2pm.

Within walking distance of the monastery along roads lined with high-priced apartments is **Palau Reial de Pedralbes**. This can provide a starting point for the tour. The Palau Reial Metro (Line 3) emerges outside the entrance to the palace grounds, which are small, formal Italianate gardens with sculptures and ponds. The Renaissance-style palace was built by the city council in 1925 to attract visits from King Alfonso XIII, who went into exile six years later and the throne room remains at the heart of the building. The **Museu de Ceràmica** and the **Museu de les Arts Decoratives** (Tues–Sun 10am–6pm; Sun 10am–3pm; entrance fee includes both museums) are housed in its

Above: the serene and lovely Pedralbes Monastery

spacious, light rooms on two floors. There are beautiful plates, pots and tiles, some from other parts of Spain, some Islamic, dating back to the 9th century. The Decorative Arts museum has a diverse collection from Renaissance furniture and painted bridal trunks to *modernista* works and 20th-century cutting-edge design.

Before it was transformed into a palace, this building was a pavilion on the holiday estate of the wealthy Güell family. The rest of the family's estate, for which Gaudí designed a lodge, stable and riding school, is situated behind the palace. Turn left outside the main gate, left up Avinguda de Pedralbes beside the Law Faculty (Barcelona's finest example of the International Style), and left again to see the Pavellons de la Finca Güell, with their magnificent entrance gate, a tortuous iron work by Gaudí featuring a dragon known as the **Drac de Pedralbes**. One pavilion houses an information centre for the Modernista Route.

Continue up Avinguda de Pedralbes to the monastery, unmissable at the top. The enclave of gold-stoned buildings is penetrated through an arch up a cobbled street. The **Museu Monestir de Pedralbes** (winter: Tues–Sat 10am–2pm; summer: 10am–5pm; Sun 10am–3pm all year; entrance fee) is on the left. The three-storey cloister is Catalan-Gothic at its most elegant. In the gardens are fruit trees, and former nuns' cells lead off around the sides. The most beautifully decorated cell belonged to the queen's niece. It was painted by Ferrer Bassa in 1346. The monastery was built for Queen Elisenda de Montcada, wife of Jaume II the Just, when she came to live here in religious isolation after his death in 1327.

In those days the sick were tended in the **infirmary**, in four rooms which now have exhibits to explain the daily lives of the Poor Clares who lived here. The **refectory** is where they ate in silence. Beside it are the kitchens, blue-tiled with stone sinks. The whole place is suffused with atmosphere.

Hidden Treasures

Since the Thyssen-Bornemisza collection moved to the MNAC (*see page 30*) the monastery has brought out hitherto unseen treasures, mostly paintings and religious artefacts.

When you leave the museum, continue up the side of the building to reach the entrance to the **church**. This simple Gothic building contains Queen Elisenda's marble tomb. Part of the nave at the back of the church, behind a grille, is used by the handful of nuns who still live in the buildings opposite the old monastery.

To return to the centre of Barcelona, turn left outside the entrance arch and follow the road down to the Reina Elisenda FGC station. Or take the No. 22 bus from Plaça de Pedralbes (left outside the monastery) to Avinguda del Tibidabo for a trip to the hilltop amusement park (see Itinerary 14, *page 53*).

Right: a painted tile in the Pedralbes cloister

12. GLORIES TO POBLE NOU *(see map, p51)*

An interesting walk off the beaten track, from the new cultural complex in Glòries to Poble Nou, an industrial area in transition, ending at the beaches beyond the Olympic Village.

Take the Plaça de les Glòries Catalanes exit from Metro Glòries for a quick look at this park created in the no-man's land of an elaborate traffic junction. A rather abandoned example of the new urban planning from the 1980s and 1990s, it is like an arena, with one exit to **Els Encants flea market** (Mon, Wed, Fri, Sat 8am–7pm) and another to the unprepossessing Glòries shopping centre, now towered over by Torre Agbar, designed by Jean Nouvel, and popularly known as the Suppository. Return to the exit leading to the Jardins del Bosquet dels Encants, a microcosmic Mediterranean wood.

Wander through to have a closer look at the **Teatre Nacional de Catalunya** (TNC), the National Theatre, opened in 1998, a larger than life neoclassical monument, designed by Ricardo Bofill. Performances are generally in Catalan, but the dance season is more accessible to visitors. Just beyond it is Rafael Moneo's **L'Auditori** opened in 1999, home of the Barcelona Orchestra (OBC) with a 2,500-seat symphonic hall and a smaller space for chamber music. The city's Music Museum is due to find a home here soon.

Industrial Relics

From this cultural complex you could head straight down the streets Pamplona or Zamora to the Olympic Village and its beaches, but for an insight into Barcelona's industrial past and present and a look at a popular neighbourhood, zig-zag down through **Poble Nou**. As the street layout has a similar grid system to the Eixample you can vary the route without fear of getting lost and be rewarded by finding gems – a timeless ironmonger's, a friendly corner bar with a cheap *menú,* a crumbling old factory with a beautiful chimney (not many left) – just keep heading down and across.

Or try this: from Avinguda Meridiana follow Bolivia for two blocks then turn right into Ávila past the new headquarters of the *mossos d'Esquadra*

(Catalonia's autonomous police force) in an enormous renovated 1930s textile factory (notice the original windows at the rear). Turn left into Tànger and on the corner of Ciutat de Granada there is a fine example of an early 20th-century wool factory, salvaged and born again with a 21st-century function as the Catalan Institute of Technology. Go down a few blocks past Restaurante Mi Casa with its tables under the plane trees. The discreet, pretty building on the corner of Carrer dels Almogàvers is the design and cutting centre of Josep Font, one of Catalonia's leading dress designers. This mixture of an industrial past (particularly in textiles: Poble Nou used to be known as the Catalan Manchester), a residue of light industry, new businesses opening, long-term residents and new apartment blocks, is fascinating. Some ruined factories are waiting to be devoured by developers; others are being carefully preserved and trendily renovated to accommodate design studios or residential lofts.

Turn left into Pallars, Pujades or Llull, and three blocks on is the gentle bustle of pretty **Rambla de Poble Nou**, with some *modernista* buildings and the atmosphere of a provincial town, with elderly folk taking the air with their grandchildren, and gossiping with their neighbours.

Follow the Rambla down towards the sea, pausing for an *orxata* or ice cream at Tio Che on the corner of Carrer del Joncar, or an excellent *tapa* at Bar Lovento (No. 21). Take a left turn into Fernando Poo to the **Plaça Prim** with its pleasing, if relatively expensive, Els Pescadors restaurant. You can get to the Mar Bella beach through the Parc Poblenou. Take a final look at the few remaining chimneys, which are rapidly being consumed by major construction: this is Diagonal Mar, a new residential area.

Return along the seafront to the Port Olímpic.

Left: the sparkling new National Theatre
Above: enjoying one of the city's beaches

13. THE BEACHES *(see pull-out map)*

Along the beaches from Barceloneta to the Port Olímpic and beyond.

The beaches that extend north from Barceloneta comprise one of the major legacies of the 1992 Olympic Games. Before the regeneration programme began, this was an industrial area to be avoided, and few people ventured here for a dip. The Vila Olímpica was planned as a smart new residential quarter and designed by various star architects. Its 2,000 apartments in six-storey blocks covering 63ha (160 acres) were first used for athletes' accommodation. The ring-road (Ronda Literal) was driven through it and the main railway line to France was hidden underground. There are more than 5km (3 miles) of sandy beaches, promenades and a leisure port lined with restaurants, while the fishing quarter of Barceloneta still has some great little bars and restaurants. Beyond the Vila Olímpica is the even newer Diagonal Mar area, centred around the site of the Forum 2004.

Old and New

Start from around **Barceloneta** Metro (Line 4), take your swimming togs, and don't forget some cash for a proper lunch. The fishing harbour is marked by a clock tower that once served as a lighthouse and nearby is the fish market (weekdays 6am and 5pm). Barceloneta was created in 1753 to house the citizens who had been usurped by the building of the Ciutadella fortress. The architect of the low-rise houses built in a grid system that allowed volleys from the castle to be directed straight down their streets, was a military engineer, Juan Martín de Cermeño, who also designed **Sant Miquel del Port**, the local church, behind which is the Barceloneta market.

The twin towers of the Arts Hotel and the MAPFRE commercial building are the highpoints of what was the Olympic Village, the housing estate that replaced the industrial wasteland. Heading along the beach or promenade

Above: the beaches at Barceloneta have been cleaned up and become fashionable

towards them, you will pass on your left, just before reaching the hospital, the singular remains of this once dusty industrial spot: a gasometer skeleton and an elaborate *modernista* **Water Tower** which was designed by Josep Domènech Estapá in 1905.

In front of the twin towers is a giant, bronze-glinting metal fish, *Pez y Esfera* by Frank Gehry, which rises above the glittering Gran Casino Barcelona at the edge of the **Port Olímpic**. Each of the quays is named after one of the local winds: Mestral, Gregal, Xaloc. Along two of them, on two levels, there are nothing but restaurants. Spilling over the quaysides are fish restaurants, ham restaurants and *tapes* bars – every kind of taste is catered for.

Beyond the port are more restaurants on the sea front, calling themselves *chirringuitos*, or shacks, a reference to the characterful beach restaurants of Barceloneta that were sacrificed during the making of the bright new seafront.

14. TIBIDABO FUNFAIR *(see map, p54)*

Via the Science Museum up to the city's lofty amusement park.

According to the Bible, the devil took Christ up into 'an exceeding high mountain and sheweth him all the kingdoms of the world, and the glory of them; And saith unto him, All these things *I will give thee* [*tibi dabo*] if thou wilt fall down and worship me.'

Tibidabo is the 517-m (1,700-ft) summit of the Collserola hills that hang behind the city. From here the view down over the world's glories, across Barcelona to the sea and the Balearic islands, north to the Pyrenees and west to Montserrat, is fantastic on about one day a year. But even with the traffic haze above the city there is a fine view of the skyline pricked by the cathedral, the Sagrada Família, the 'Suppository' and the skyscrapers of the Olympic village. An afternoon or evening out here can be a family occasion, taking in Tibidabo's amusement park and having hands-on fun at CosmoCaixa, the Science Museum.

Getting up the hill is part of the pleasure. The No 123 bus takes you straight there, but the more adventurous will take the FGC train Line 7 from Plaça Catalunya to Avinguda Tibidabo station, to emerge at the Tramvia Blau (blue tram) stop outside Hospital Sant Gervasi, the former Rotonda Hotel with a *modernista* minaret.

For the **CosmoCaixa** (Tues–Sun 10am–8pm; entrance fee), the newly renovated science museum, walk up the Avinguda del Tibidabo past some dramatic 19th-century mansions,

Right: the ornate Sagrat Cor church on top of Tibidabo

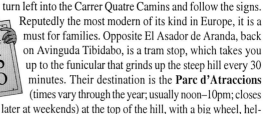

turn left into the Carrer Quatre Camins and follow the signs. Reputedly the most modern of its kind in Europe, it is a must for families. Opposite El Asador de Aranda, back on Avinguda Tibidabo, is a tram stop, which takes you up to the funicular that grinds up the steep hill every 30 minutes. Their destination is the **Parc d'Atraccions** (times vary through the year; usually noon–10pm; closes later at weekends) at the top of the hill, with a big wheel, helter skelter and white-knuckle rides, including the Pasaje del Terror and the Avion Tibiair, a red aeroplane that swoops off the side of the hill into empty space. There is also a museum of mechanical toys. The entrace fee includes all rides on the six levels of hillside attractions.

City Views

It is not obligatory to visit the funfair on Tibidabo. There are restaurants on the hill, with fine views, and pleasant paths to walk. Above is the **Sagrat Cor**, the Sacred Heart church, a 20th-century confection that grew from a 19th-century retreat of a hermit, Sant Joan Bosco. A lift inside the church gives a lofty view of the city. For another view, take the lift up to the glassed-in observation platform on the 10th floor of the nearby 288-m (945-ft) **Torre Collserola** communications tower (Mon–Fri 11am–2.30pm, 3.30–8pm; all day at weekends). Designed by British architect Sir Norman Foster, this is sometimes known locally as Torre Foster.

You can also use Tibidabo as local people do, as a retreat from the city. It crowns the Collserola massif, some 8,000ha (19,700 ares) of woodland, where you can walk, cycle, picnic, or explore typical Catalan country houses.

Above: an inviting, old-fashioned sign at the museum of mechanical toys
Right: all the fun of the fair

Excursions

1. SITGES *(see pull-out map)*

The first man in Spain to pursue swimming as a leisure activity was the fin-de-siècle artist Santiago Rusiñol. He took the plunge in Sitges, a pretty fishing village 40km (25 miles) south of Barcelona, and anyone in the city in summer today will feel a need to follow his example.

Although the best known of the capital's local resorts, easily reached in a day trip, **Sitges** remains a pretty and civilised place. A former wine town which had trade links with America, it prospered in the 19th century, when so-called Indianos, local people who had gone abroad to find their fortune, had come home wealthy to retire in mansions and build summer houses. Barcelona's new bourgeoisie found their way here, too. The Luminist School of Sitges preceded Rusiñol and the Modernists, but when this energetic artist and writer bought his home here in 1891, Sitges was dubbed by the Barcelona press as 'the Mecca of Modernism'. Later, the Spanish poet and playwright Federico García Lorca (1899–1936) came to stay, as did the French composer Erik Satie (1866–1925). Subsequent regular visitors included the English writer G.K. Chesterton (1874–1936), to whom the town has erected a statue. In the late 1950s and early 1960s Sitges responded to the coast's great tourist influx by providing a wide range of pubs and bars and a few hotels; local people rented out rooms in summer and a few entrepreneurs built modest apartment blocks, but no high-rises followed and, in the main, development has been contained.

Getting There

The resort is highly accessible from the capital. The A16 motorway (toll) has been blasted through the Garraf mountains to alleviate the congested *autovia* that winds along by the sea south from Barcelona. Trains leave from the central Sants or Passeig de Gràcia stations every 30 minutes. Fast trains take 25 minutes; others, stopping at nearly every station, take almost twice as long. If possible avoid summer weekends, when the town is at its busiest.

Like most resorts on the coast, it has several beaches. Sant Sebastià is to the north; further south are the Platjes dels Morts, two nude beaches, one for heterosexuals, one for gays. The main beach, however, the **Platja d'Or**, is the great attraction, and the visitor should head straight down to it from the station. The clean sandy strand is 5km (3 miles) long, backed by a palm-lined promenade and overlooked from the north by the distinctive facade of the 17th-century church, Sant Bartomeu i Santa Tecla.

The liveliest thoroughfare is **Carrer Primer de Maig**, which runs back from the middle of the promenade. This street of bars is known as the **Carrer**

Left: stunning colours in the Museu Maricel
Right: tourist information in Sitges

del **Pecat** (Sin Street) and it is here that Sitges' main annual festivities reach their height. At Corpus Christi (in May or June) carpets of flowers cover the street, but its most vibrant time is during pre-Lent carnival, when there is an elaborate show of costume and design. The Shrove Tuesday evening parade is the most outrageous, when transvestites take centre stage.

At the top of Primer de Maig turn right and then left up Carrer Sant Josep to find the **Museu Romàntic** (summer: Tues–Fri 9.30am–1.30pm, 4–9pm; winter: 9.30am–1.30pm, 3–6.30pm; Sat–Sun 10am–5pm all year; entrance fee, guided visits on the hour) on the corner of Carrer Sant Gaudenci. This house, built in 1793 by the cultured Llopis family, was given to the town complete as a contemporary museum of family life. The top floor has a large collection of dolls amassed by the local children's writer Lola Anglada.

Return down Sant Josep and turn left into Carrer Parellades and continue down to Carrer Major – or take any agreeable little street down towards the distinctive church at the top end of the beach. A cannon here bears a plaque explaining that it saw off two English frigates that had their eyes on cargo ships anchored in the bay. Behind the church in Carrer Fonoller magnificent white mansions seem to belong to an affluent city rather than a seaside resort.

Rusiñol's Home

On the left is the **Palau Maricel**, with a roof terrace of lovely blue tiles. Used by the local council, it may be visited in summer. On the right is the entrance to the **Museu Maricel** (Jul–Sept: 10am–2pm, 5–9pm; Oct–Jun: 10am–1.30pm, 3–6.30pm; Sun 10am–3pm all year; entrance fee). This former hospital was renovated by the critic and artist, Miquel Utrillo, a founder, along with Rusiñol and Casas, of Barcelona's Quatre Gats café *(see page 39)*. This museum is taken up with a collection of Gothic paintings and furniture

Above: the distinctive facade of Sitges' main church lords it over the crowded beach

and has a room decorated by Josep Luís Sert. It is also the home of the town's important art collection, with works by the Romantics, Luminists and Modernists who were associated with Sitges.

The neighbouring building is **Cau Ferrat** (same opening hours), home of Santiago Rusiñol. Like many artists of his generation, he was funded by his family – his had grown rich in Barcelona's industrial revolution. He travelled frequently to Paris, forging important links for local artists. He bought fishermen's cottages here to turn into a mansion to house his collection of ironwork, sculptures and paintings and to use as a studio. Between 1892 and 1899 he put on the *Festes Modernistes*, art festivals with concerts, plays and dance. The collection is a bright and cheerful and is just as he left it, including his own bed. There are two El Grecos (bought in Paris, they were carried through the town like venerated statues in a mock Holy Week procession), five small Picassos and an intriguing double portrait painted by both Rusiñol and Ramón Casas, Modernist painting's other great exponent.

North of these imposing buildings is **Sant Sebastià** beach. Quieter than the main beach, it offers good restaurants, with pavement cafés. But there are also plenty of restaurants, bars and chic shops to visit along the main waterfront, around the Carrer Primer de Maig, and in pretty back streets.

2. CAVA COUNTRY *(see pull-out map)*

An excursion 40km (25 miles) south of Barcelona into the Penedès wine-producing region. (Note that many wine houses close in August.)

Catalonia's gift to the world's table is *Cava*, a sparkling wine produced in exactly the same way as Champagne, but forbidden the French appellation by the EU and the lawyers from Rheims. The ruling of the European courts is likely to turn out to be in the wine's favour, for the word *Cava* has been seeping into foreign languages as a word that means very good, inexpensive, earthy, non-acid sparkling wine. Around 90 percent of the country's output comes from the Penedès region, to the south of Barcelona, in vineyards around the towns of Vilafranca del Penedès and Sant Sadurní d'Anoia.

Some travel agencies and tour operators organise visits to the producers, though the most comprehensive information on visits to the over 300 wine and *Cava* producers in the area is the Vilafranca Tourist Office (Cort 14; www.ajvilafranca.es). However, it is also perfectly possible to visit both towns independently in a day out, and gain a flavour not just of the product but of the countryside. Leaving Barcelona, take the A7 motorway which passes both towns, or a RENFE train to Vilafranca, which leave Plaça Catalunya and Sants stations every hour taking 45 minutes to **Sant Sadurní d'Anoia**. where a bacchanalian tour can begin. Beside the station is the **Freixenet** house, one of the largest

LA PLAÇA MÉS CASTELLERA

Right: wall tiles in Vilafranca celebrate the *castellers*

in the region, which has regular tours throughout the day (tel: 93 891 7000). More impressive is the out-of-town **Codorníu** house, which also has tours (93 818 3232), signposted and about 20 minutes' walk from the station. This is the home of *Cava*. Josep Raventós, of the Cordoníu family dynasty, popped the first *Cava* cork here in 1872. His son Manuel took over the firm 13 years later after the vine phylloxera louse had devastated the region. He replanted and rebuilt the vineyards and buildings, adding the huge *modernista* cellars designed by Puig i Cadafalch and now a national monument with a museum and related posters of graphic art. The tour of the cellars includes an explanation of the wine making and a train ride through part of the five storeys of cellars that cover 26km (16 miles).

Sant Sadurní is a small country town without much activity. A plaque on the town hall commemorates a visit by King Juan Carlos and Queen Sofía in 1987, on the centenary of the first *Cava* production after the phylloxera blight had been eradicated.

Human Pyramids

For lunch it may be best to head on to the tranquil old town of **Vilafranca del Penedès** some 15 minutes further down the line by train, a little longer by bus. There are some excellent restaurants around the town as you might expect, some with plaques showing they are on the Rute del Vi i del Cava. More simply, you can sit at the marble-topped tables in the pretty **Cafe el Coro** in the **Plaça de la Villa**: This square, where you can find the town hall and tourist office, has wall tiles celebrating the *castellers*, human pyramids that are a custom of the region. They gather here at the end of August and, physically supported by the crowds, compete for height, balance and skill. '*Hi ha Cava a copes*' all the bars proclaim: 'There is *Cava* by the glass here'. But in fact Vilafranca is the centre for still wine production. The old *bodega* of the

great **Torres** family is at 22 Carrer de Commercio, beside the station, though you can also visit their state-of-the-art winery out of town. The tourist office has a list of producers that can be visited, as does the **Museu del Vi**, Spain's best wine museum (summer: Tues–Sat 9am–9pm, Sun 10am–2pm; winter: 10am–2pm, 4–7pm; entrance fee includes tasting). The museum occupies a former palace of the count-kings of Catalonia-Aragon in the Plaça Jaume I, opposite the basilica of Santa Maria. It has various implements from the industry's past, and a bar displays the region's wine. There is a also a collection of ceramics and archaeology.

If you have your own transport, you can visit **Sitges**, 22km (14 miles) south on the coast *(see Excursion 1, page 57)*. There is also a bus service, but there is no rail link.

Left: a market in Sant Sadurní

3. Discovering Dali *(see pull-out map)*

A trip to Dalí country, beginning in Figueres, about 1½ hours' drive from Barcelona, then on to Port Lligat some 30 km/18 miles away, returning via the castle of Púbol, near Girona. Figueres is accessible by train but you need private transport and an overnight stop if you want to visit all three sites.

The art treasures of Barcelona, ancient and modern, often engender an interest in Catalunya's most extravagant artist, the Surrealist Salvador Dalí. This excursion takes you to three museums dedicated to his life and work (www.salvador-dali.org). The first is in the market town of **Figueres**, where the artist was born in 1904, the son of a public notary. Many of his major works are displayed in the **Teatre-Museu Dalí** (Jul–Sept: daily 9am–7.15pm; Oct–Jun: Tues–Sun 10.30am–5.15pm; entrance fee). Set in the Plaça Gala-Salvador Dalí, to the north of the town's main rambla, the museum was constructed on the site of a municipal theatre that was burned down in 1939, at the end of the Civil War. Dalí died in the adjoining Torre Galatea in 1989 and he is buried in the crypt.

Among the extraordinary works here are the *Poetry of America*, or *Cosmic Athletes*, painted in 1943, a portrait of Gala as *Atomic Leda*, and the huge ceiling fresco dominating the *Wind Palace Room* on the first floor. In the garden, the *Rainy Taxi* sculpture is a crowd puller. This is one of the few art galleries that small children generally enjoy – its quirkiness appeals to their sense of the ridiculous.

It is advisable to avoid visiting the museum on a Thursday morning when there is a large market in the town – though the market is fun to visit, it makes it very difficult to park. Wet or cloudy days, when people are forced off the beaches in search of entertainment, see the longest queues.

To Cadaqués

From Figueres it's about 30 km (18 miles) to **Cadaqués**, a pretty fishing village made famous by Dalí. Nearby is Port Lligat, the tiny port where he and his wife Gala lived for many years in a house comprising several fishermen's cottages joined together.

As you drive down the hill towards the **Casa-Museu Dalí** you will see the Castor and Pollux heads and the large sculpted eggs on the roof – the

Right: the Teatre-Museu Dalí in Figueres

latter feature repeated on the Torre Galatea (mid-Jun–mid-Sept: Tues–Sun 10.30am–9pm; mid-Sept–1 Nov and mid-Mar–mid-Jun: 10.30am–6pm; entrance fee; it is essential to book in advance because people are only allowed into the museum in small, carefully regulated groups; tel: 97 225 1015). Set in a garden of gnarled olive trees, the house offers a wonderful insight into the unusual domestic life of the Dalís. Huge windows frame views of the harbour and the Mediterranean, and in the Yellow Room a mirror is angled so that Dalí, in bed in the open-plan adjoining room, could see the light of the rising sun. Gala's touch is visible in many areas, particularly in the Room of the Cupboards where she covered cupboard doors with photos and magazine covers of special interest; and in the 'everlasting flowers' with which she festooned the windows. The swimming pool area is a marvellous example of Dalían kitsch. The pool itself, modelled on one at the Alhambra in Granada, shares space with a statue of Diana the Huntress and models of Michelin men and Pirelli tyres.

You could spend the night in the Hotel Port Lligat, almost next door to the house, where there's a pleasant restaurant and an excellent swimming pool (tel: 97 225 8162), or in one of the small hotels in Cadaques.

The next day, return to Figueres where you can either take the motorway towards Girona, and turn onto the C-255 shortly before the city, or take a slower route on a pleasant side road (C-252 in the direction of the pottery town of La Bisbal) and look for signs to the **Castell Gala-Dalí** at Púbol (Jun–Sept: daily 10.30am–8pm; Mar–Jun and Oct–Nov: Tues–Sun 10.30am–6pm; entrance fee). The castle is 4.5 km (2½ miles) from Flaça railway station and 2km (1 mile) from the nearest bus stop.

Dalí restored this Gothic-Renaissance castle and gave it to Gala in 1970, promising only to enter it at her invitation. He painted frescoes in the interior and built the crypt where Gala is buried. He moved to the castle on the day of her death in 1982 and stayed, becoming increasingly frail, until a fire two years later obliged him to move to the Torre Galatea in Figueres.

4. THE HOLY MOUNTAIN *(see pull-out map)*

Montserrat, the serrated mountain, is Barcelona's most holy shrine. Its blunt, grey rocky walls rise to a sheer 1,241m (4,075ft) and extend over 50 sq km (18 sq miles) making it not only visible for miles around, but also easily identified on flights in and out of Barcelona airport.

Displayed in the 16th-century basilica of the monastic complex is the Black Virgin of Montserrat, La Moreneta, a Romanesque statue of the Madonna and Child that has been the subject of great veneration. Catalans are not especially known for their devoutness, and this statue and her mountain have captured their imagination for political as much as for religious reasons. In her rocky stronghold, La Moreneta is looked to for protection against invaders and tyrants. Her elected abbot is seen as an upholder of Catalan liberties. Catalans are expected to make a pilgrimage to this holy mountain once in their lives and its choir is famous the world over.

A cloudy or overcast day will hamper the wonderful views, and be warned that the weather at this height can be changeable, cold and turbulent.

Getting There

Montserrat lies 50km (30 miles) inland, 45 minutes by car along the new autovia to Martorell. FGC trains run from Plaça Espanya every hour and take one hour either to the **Aeri de Montserrat** station, where a cable car takes five minutes to reach the monastery or, more comfortably, the next stop, **Monistrol de Montserrat**, where the Cremallera rack-and-pinion train takes 15 minutes. Either way the ticket costs the same.

At the monastery, visitors' needs are catered for with shops, cafés, restaurants and stalls selling delicious local cheeses and honey. The information office opposite the Cremallera train station has an exhibition that gives an account of the lives of the benedictine monks who still live here. Steps then lead up to the main square and **basilica**. The monastery became a Benedictine establishment in AD967, but everything about it today is rather new. Its most recent destruction was in 1811 during the Napoleonic wars when, after a stout defence by Catalan guerillas, its treasures were plundered and its library burned. The monks did not return for more than 50 years and the basilica was given its present facade in 1900.

The abbey is open 6am–8pm, but the time to arrive is when the boys' choir, which has had a school here since the 13th century, sings (daily 1pm, 6.45pm; closed July and 26 Dec–8 Jan). Behind them, above the

Left: Casa-Museu Dalí at Port Lligat
Right: the monastery courtyard

altar, is **La Moreneta** herself. There is a separate door at the front of the basilica for people wanting to see and touch this statue of Madonna and Child, blackened by centuries of candle smoke. The legend is that it was made by St Luke and brought to Barcelona by St Peter. All manner of royalty and nobility have pledged themselves to her. St Ignatius Loyola, founder of the Jesuits, dedicated himself to her service.

Outside the basilica in the Plaça de Santa Maria is the **museum** (daily 9.30am–6pm), with ecclesiastical treasures and archaeology from Egypt, plus Roman and Byzantine ceramics. It also has a 19th- and 20-century art collection, including works by Dalí, Degas, Monet, Picasso and Sisley and the Catalan schools. Caravaggio, El Greco and Tiepolo are also represented.

The Way of the Cross

There are a number of excursions to be made from the monastery. **Via Crucis**, the Way of the Cross, is behind the Plaça de l'Abat Oliba. Its modern statues lead to the hermitage of Sant Miquel. From Plaça de la Creu a cable car runs down to **Santa Cova**. This chapel is in a grotto where the Virgin is said to have been hidden during the Moorish occupation. But a clear day may demand a more spectacular excursion. **Sant Joan** is one of the mountain's 13 small *ermitas* inhabited by hermits until Napoleon's troops, having hanged the monks, hunted them down 'like wild goats' and killed them.

Behind the funicular station in Plaça Santa Creu is another, which takes passengers up to the hermitage. There is a café and restaurant where it stops, then a 20-minute walk up to the hermitage. From here it is possible to walk to **Sant Jeroni**, the highest point of the mountain.

Anyone who stays longer than they intended might like to know that there are two places to stay in the monastery: the Cel.les Abat Marcet and the 3-star Abat Cisernos. For all information about Montserrat, tel: 93 877 7701.

Above: the monastery at Montserrat. **Left:** La Moreneta
Right: the mountain road climbs steeply to the top

Leisure Activities

SHOPPING

Barcelona is an enormously attractive place to shop, from its innovative, designer-conscious showcases around Passeig de Gràcia and Diagonal to the bright lights of the port's Maremàgnum and the delightful little specialist shops that seem to have remained virtually unchanged for years in the sunless streets of the Barri Gòtic. Any shopping spree can be punctuated by sights of *Modernista* or Gothic architecture, and relieved by regular refreshment at pavement cafés or *tapes* bars.

Barcelona's fame has spread and people come a long way to buy fashionable clothes, leather bags and shoes; ceramics, especially earthenware, wickerwork, knives, scissors, stationery, perfumes, candles, dried flowers, lacework, antiques, prints and designer objects. That is to say nothing of the abundance of tempting and transportable food, from nuts and dried fruit to olives and virgin olive oil, available in markets and *colmados*, the wonderful old grocers' found in every neighbourhood. Or chocolates from specialist makers.

Less attractive but ever-practical are the department stores and shopping centres: the long-established El Corte Inglés, with branches in Plaça Catalunya and Avinguda Diagonal and the latest one, specialising in music, books and sport, in Portal de l'Angel (open 10am–9.30pm), is the town's busiest department store.

Avinguda Portal de l'Angel is a lively shopping street, good for shoes and young fashion, running down from the Plaça Catalunya towards the cathedral, and turning into the equally lively Portaferrissa shopping street on the right at the bottom, which leads to La Rambla.

More fashionable and more fun than the department stores are the shopping malls. Bulevar Rosa was the first to open, in 1968, and remains one of the best (there are branches in Passeig de Gràcia and Diagonal). Gralla Hall in Portaferrissa is very hip. Relatively new are the huge shopping centres like El Triangle in Plaça Catalunya, which is known for its high-tech FNAC store, and L'Illa at Diagonal 545–57, an upmarket choice.

The latest and largest in Catalonia, La Maquinista, controversially replaced an enormous old factory in Sant Andreu (open from 10am–10pm). The large mall out in Diagonal Mar is another place for big-shop dallying. For late night shopping try VIPS in Rambla de Catalunya 7–9, with shops and cafés, or Maremàgnum in the harbour, where fashion shops are open until 11pm, when you can move straight into the discos.

Eixample Chic

Designer clothes, designer furniture, designer stores… the Eixample is where the cutting edge of Barcelona's fashion lies, even though it is now being challenged by alternative movements in the Born and El Raval districts of the Old Town, where secondhand clothes and offbeat designs have become acceptable, and more upmarket designers are moving in.

Left: a chic shop in the Eixample
Right: El Raval's new shopkeepers

Take the Eixample street by street: some shops are worth visiting just for window shopping and for a peek at their stylish interiors. Designer names to look out for include Antonio Miró, Josep Font, Armand Basi, David Valls, Lluís Generó and Purificación Garcia. Popular local chain stores include Massimo Dutti, Mango and the extremely successful Zara, the phenomenon of the nineties, where men, women and children can always find some solution to a clothing crisis.

Passeig de Gràcia: coming up from Plaça Catalunya, at No 4 is a revamped Gonzalo Comella, favoured by the up-town crowd, with their own and international labels; then for classic, stylish male fashion there's Furest at No 14, followed by Zara's flagship store in a spectacular building on the corner of Gran Via.

On the other side at No 35 is Loewe, for smart leatherware. Bulevar Rosa, the forerunner of Barcelona's malls, with some 70 shops, sells mostly fashion, and leather bags. At the Centre Català d'Artesania there are three rooms showing new local craft work. At No 89, Adolfo Dominguez, leading Spanish designer of classic fashion, has kitted out his own store. Just after Gaudí's La Pedrera, with an excellent souvenir shop, is Vinçon, the interior design store that is not to be missed.

Consell de Cent, just off Passeig de Gràcia, is the latest stylish domain of Barcelona's fashion king, Antonio Miró (no relation to the artist), something of a trailblazer in the late 1960s and still a leader. Men and women are both catered for.

Another street off this main avenue that is well worth checking out is Rosselló, where Dos y Una at No 275, is an up-market souvenir shop with creative gift ideas, like their Spanish bull pan scourer. At No 271, La Inmaculada Concepción specialises in all kinds of *Modernista* fixtures and fittings, and opposite is Z..Z..Vinçon, devoted to snoozing and bedrooms.

Rambla de Catalunya is full of interesting shopping possibilities and makes a pleasant walk. Muxart at No 47 is the subtlest shop front in a *Modernista* building, and sells very classy Catalan-designed shoes and bags. Or from the top of Passeig de Gràcia, you could go up Diagonal, where the shops become increasingly exclusive: at No 403, Pilma is a highly popular and sophisticated modern furniture shop that also sells wonderful objets d'art. No 466, Eleven, is a shoe shop with a striking modern interior designed by Manuel Ybarguengoitia and Maria del Mar Nogués.

Jean Pierre Bua at No 469, with a metal and concrete interior designed by Eduard Samsó, is where you will find all Spain's top designer names and international labels. Try No 598, Sara Navarra, for good, inexpensive shoes and leatherware, and keep on up for L'Illa.

Gothic Antiquities

There are some wonderful old shops in the Gothic quarter, and this is the best place to look for antiques and second-hand books as well as new fashion and interior design, and second-hand shops.

Behind the cathedral is a narrow street, Carrer Freneria, with Grafiques el Tinell at No.1, specialising in lithographs and old prints, particularly posters of blocks of the old guild *(gremis)* trades and crafts usually seen in decorative tiles. Next door La Caixa de Fang sells a fine range of earthenware. Around the corner at No. 7 Llibreteria is an ancient candle shop, Cereria Subirà and towards Plaça Sant Jaume there's a colourful mixture of fashion and souvenir shops.

Cross the Plaça to Carrer del Call in the old Jewish quarter and follow it to the end, where you'll find Obach, for any kind of hat, especially a huge range of berets. This magnificent shop is on the corner of Banys Nous, where there are several attractive shops: at No 5 Gemma Povo stocks antiques including wrought iron, furniture and hand-blown glass, and Instinto has its own designs, stylish women's clothes in comfortable fabrics and jewellery. Germanes Garcia situated on the corner of Ave María is the best place to buy baskets and anything you could wish for in wicker, from desks to lampshades.

Plaça de Sant Josep Oriol: Joguines Monfort is a treasure trove of toys, and Coses del Casa is good for fabrics. Carrer Petritxol, off Plaça del Pi, is full of jewellers and art galleries (Dalmau, who was Picasso and Miró's agent, operated from here). No 2, Libreria Quera, is the place to go for maps and photography books about the Catalan countryside. Plaça del Pi has Roca, a magnificent knife shop selling every kind of blade.

Shopping is a pleasant experience in the Born area where attractive small shops are opening constantly.

Markets

The big flea market is Els Encants in Plaça de les Glòries (Metro Line I). It's fun but most of it really is junk. It's held on Monday, Wednesday, Friday and Saturday from 8am–8pm; 7pm in winter.

An antique market is held in the cathe-

dral square (Thursday), and country produce is sold in the Plaça del Pi during the week. Painters sell their work in neighbouring Plaça Sant Josep Oriol at weekends. A stamp and coin market is held in the Plaça Reial from 9am–2.30pm on Sunday, worth visiting for the atmosphere.

Stamps, books and video games are on sale in Sant Antoni market from 9am–2pm on Sunday. The market is to the west of the Rambla at the far end of Carrer del Carme, continuing along Carrer de Sant Antoni Abat. Every weekend the lower part of La Rambla holds an arts and crafts fair, and on the other side of the Columbus monument is a bric-à-brac market.

Gifts and souvenirs

La Rambla is disappointing for shopping, apart from the newsstands, which are a feast of magazines and newspapers. Tacky souvenir shops sell Barça football memorabilia (which can also be bought at the Camp Nou's own shop), but one place, La Botiga de la Virreina, at No 99, makes up for them all with stylish goods and books, designed in or about Barcelona.

The attractive museum shops are another excellent source of gifts and temptation. The ones that particularly stand out are the shops at the Textile Museum, the history museums, and the MACBA.

Left: Els Encants flea market
Above: a shop selling classic comics

EATING OUT

As in any civilised society, *barcelonins* are quite serious about their food. 'Where did you eat?' they will ask with uncharacteristic interest, and you know your reply will mark you out either as a person of taste and distinction or as someone who needs taking in hand. Catalan cuisine is an ancient Mediterranean cuisine, full of the aromas of mountain herbs, the oils and the juices of the plains, the wild meat of the woods and skies, and the flesh of the fish and crustaceans of the sea. *Mar i montanya* is how it is described, a special mixture of seafood and meat. The first cook book ever written in Europe was the Catalan *Llibre de Sant Sovi* of 1324.

Other cuisines can be tried in the city and there is no shortage of places to eat. The smarter restaurants in the Eixample or up-town may have some of the best food, but they tend to lack the personality of the old town where some great old establishments such as Agut, Caracoles and Set Portes rub shoulders with newer, trendier places *(see below for some recommendations).*

Lunch is the best value, eaten from 2–4pm, when most restaurants have inexpensive three-course set menus with wine. An average à la carte may turn out to be twice the price. Dinner is eaten at about 10pm. Typically a meal will begin with an *amanida catalana*, a salad with cold meats; or *escalivada*, baked peppers and aubergines,

skinned, covered in oil and eaten cold; or *esqueixada*, a salad with shredded cod. A main course could be a *suquet*, fish stew or *estofat*, meat stew; or *botifarra amb mongetes*, sausage and beans; or rabbit, *conill*, served with snails *(cargols)* or with a garlicky *allioli* sauce. For dessert, *crema catalana*, a local *crème brulée*, is essential.

Alternatively, just a few portions *(racions)* or a smaller amount *(tapes)* can be filling, especially when eaten with a chunk of Catalonia's best invention, *pa amb tomàquet*, bread rubbed with garlic, fruity olive oil and tomato. Have it with ham *(pernil)*, spicy sausage *(xoriço)*, cheese *(formatge)* or anchovies *(anxoves)*.

Other dishes to point to on the bar might include *truites,* omelettes made with potato and onion or with spinach; small fried fish; octopus; snails; or *patates braves*, potatoes in a hot tomato sauce.

Typical menu items
Entrants/Primer plat **Starter/First course**
Amanida **Green salad**
Empedrat **White bean salad with tomatoes, onions, salt cod, olives**
Espinacs a la catalana **Steamed spinach lightly fried with raisins and pine nuts**
Sopa de peix **Fish soup**
Gaspatxo **Andalucian cold tomato soup**
Escudella **Thick soup with noodles, the stock left from boiling meat**
Arros negre **Black rice, squid and its ink**

Above: eating outdoors on a warm summer evening

Cigrons **Chick peas, often stewed with chard** (*bledes*), **spinach, tiny clams or cod**
Llenties **Lentils, usually with spicy sausage and black pudding**
Faves a la catalana **Broad beans, stewed as lentils**
Verdures **Vegetable of the day, often overcooked with potatoes**
Canelons a la barcelonina **Cannelloni stuffed with meat**
Croquetes cassolanes **Home made croquettes (chicken, ham or salt cod)**

Segon plat **Main course**
Pollastre/Carn arrebossada **Chicken/meat (usually beef) fried in breadcrumbs**
Peix (lluç, tonyina, gambes, sèpia…) a la planxa **Fish (hake, tuna, prawns, cuttlefish) cooked on a griddle. Meat or rabbit also cooked this way**
Calamars a la romana/farcits **Squid fried in batter/stuffed**
Mandonguilles **Meatballs**
Xai a la brasa **Lamb cooked on open wood or charcoal fire**
Fetge **Liver**
Pollastre rostit **Chicken roasted in a rich sauce**
Fricandó **Braised veal with wild mushrooms**
Salsitxes amb tomàquet **Thin sausages in tomato sauce**

Postres **Desserts**
Fruite (Poma, platan, pressec, sindria) **Fresh fruit (apple, banana, peach, watermelon etc)**
Macedonia **Fruit salad**
Flam **Crème caramel**
Postre de music **Nuts and dried fruits, often served with moscatel (sweet wine)**
Pastis **Tart/cake**
Gelat **Ice cream**
Mel i mató **Curd cheese with honey**

Where to Eat

Going for *tapes* can be a source of great fun in the **Barri Gòtic**, in the bars whose lights spill out on to the narrow medieval lanes. Carrer Mercè, behind Passeig de Colom has a good choice.

In the Eixample it is a smarter affair, with some traditional bars and modern *cervecerias* such as Tapa Tapa, Passeig de Gracia 44, where the tempting dishes line the bars. A new wave of Basque *tapes* bars are all over town. Try Irati, Cardenal Casanyas, 17, one of the first and best.

The **port** is a favourite area for eating, and there is no lack of restaurants along the quayside, particularly at the Palau de Mar, a good place for people-watching, in Passeig Joan de Borbó and in the intimate local streets of Barceloneta. Salmonete in the **Maremàgnum** is the new site of the popular *chirringuito* restaurant that was torn down from the beach in Barceloneta. Others moved to the **Olympic Port**, where diners are spoilt for choice. Familiar names from Barceloneta, such as El Rey de la Gamba, jostle with new fish restaurants.

Wines of the region are good, and unless you know what you are doing, stick to the house wine. Red is often served cold, which can improve the rougher stuff. White-wine drinkers might like to try the pinks (*rosat*), which can be very refreshing.

The Penedès wine region just to the south also produces champagne-method wines called *Cava*, which is a little more expensive than still wine. A small bottle of it, a *benjamin*, is a pleasant drink to have in a bar any time of day.

Recommendations

Many restaurants are closed on Sunday night and Monday, and some take an annual holiday in August. Even expensive restaurants offer good value set menus at lunch-time, or try a *menú de degustació*, a selection of their best food.

The Eixample *(Expensive)*
Botafumeiro
Carrer Gran de Gràcia 81
Tel: 93 218 4230
Frequently described as the greatest seafood place in town. Plus oyster bar. €€€

Jaume de Provença
Carrer de Provença 88
Tel: 93 430 0029
A cool, modern ambience is appropriate for one of Barcelona's leading *nouvelle cuisine* Catalan restaurants. €€€

Tragaluz
Passatge de la Concepció 5
Tel: 93 487 0621
Creative Mediterranean cuisine under large skylight. Spectacular Mariscal-designed loos. *Tapes* downstairs from 8.30pm. €€€

The Eixample *(Moderate)*
Casa Alfonso
Roger de Llúria 6
Tel: 93 301 9783
The restaurant in this well-established bar specialises in grilled meat, but the fun is eating Alfonso's excellent ham and other snacks at the bar. €€

El Japonés
Passatge de la Concepció 2
Tel: 93 487 2592
Trendy place for sushi. Stunning minimalist décor in this offspring of Tragaluz. €€

Madrid-Barcelona
Aragó 282
Tel: 93 215 7026
Renovating this classic old restaurant luckily didn't affect the bustling atmosphere or the good traditional dishes. Conveniently situated just off Passeig de Gràcia. €€

The Old Town *(Expensive)*
Casa Leopoldo
Carrer de Sant Rafael 24
Tel: 93 441 3014
This is a family-run classic in the narrow streets of the Barri Xines, renowned for its fish. €€€

Can Majó
Carrer d'Almirall Aixada 23
Tel: 93 221 5455
One of the best and most established fish restaurants in the newly revitalised Barceloneta area. Good paella. €€€

El Suquet de l'Almirall
Passeig Joan de Borbó 65
Tel: 93 221 6233
An attractive, low-key restaurant with a small pavement terrace overlooking the yachts, this is one of the finest places to eat in Barceloneta with excellent, creative seafood dishes. €€€

Gran Café
Carrer d'Avinyó 9
Tel: 93 318 7986
Smart, nostalgic decor, in a grand old former sewing-machine shop. €€

Hofmann
Argenteria, 74–8
Tel: 93 319 5889
Close to Santa Maria del Mar church, renowned chef Mey Hofmann's restaurant is a place for gourmets, recently awarded a Michelin star. Don't miss the exquisite *postres.*€€€

Set Portes
Passeig d'Isabel II, 14
Tel: 93 319 3033
Many well-known names have dined here over the years, including Picasso and Lorca. Founded in 1836, it's a Barcelona institution and a worthy one. Seafood and rice dishes are its specialities. €€€

The Old Town *(Moderate)*
Cafè de L'Acadèmia
Lledó 1
Tel: 93 315 0026
Refreshingly different Catalan dishes in pleasant surroundings, with candle-lit outdoor tables set in a Gothic square. Closed at weekends. €€

Can Lluís
Carrer Cera 49
Tel: 93 441 6081
Out of the way and intimate, this little restaurant serves good local food. €€

Els Quatre Gats
Montsió 3
Tel: 93 302 4140
The café Puig i Cadafalch built and which the artists frequented has been restored, and though maybe not the best food in town, it's fun to sit where they all sat. €€

Freud B'Art
Baixada de Sant Miquel 4
Tel: 93 318 6629
Cool cocktails and decor lead into equally stylish and creative food in this relaxing restaurant that doubles as art gallery. €€

Left: *esqueixada* is a Catalan speciality

Los Caracoles
Carrer dels Escudellers 14
Tel: 93 302 3185
This is another Gothic quarter institution. This has just the kind of atmosphere one imagines an old Barcelona restaurant should have. It is popular with tourists, but well worth a visit. €€

Rita Blue
Plaça de Sant Agustí 3
Tel: 93 42 4086
The local saint of the impossible has given her name to this fun, trendy bar/restaurant with excellent fusion food. €€

Santa Maria
Carrer del Comerç 17
Tel: 93 315 1227
Serving new-generation Catalan food in delicate amounts, this attractive small restaurant has become very trendy. Delicious, exciting flavours. €€

Senyor Parellada
Argenteria 37,
Tel: 93 310 5094
Stylish brasserie with great atmosphere; new and traditional Catalan dishes. €€

Taxidermista
Plaça Reial 8
Tel: 93 412 4536
Snacky Mediterranean food is served in this good-looking café-cum-restaurant in the square. It is named after its former owner's occupation. €€

The Old Town *(Inexpensive)*
Egipte
La Rambla 79
Tel: 93 317 9545
A great bistro-type establishment that's been around for years, with value-for-money dishes served in antique-filled rooms. €

El Portalón
Banys Nous 20
Tel: 93 302 1187
A good value *menú del día*, pitchers of rough red wine and locals playing dominoes. It's a real gem. The winter bean stews are especially good. €

La Cassola
Carrer de Sant Sever 3
Tel: 93 318 1580
Welcoming family-run restaurant with good home cooking and Catalan specialities. €

La Dolça Herminia
Magdalenes 27
Tel: 93 317 0676
Unusual dishes in a surprisingly reasonable fixed menu amid soothing, sophisticated décor, just off the busy Via Laietana. €

Iposa
Floristes de la Rambla 14
Tel: 93 318 6086
Tucked behind the Boqueria market. Creative dishes, young crowd. €

Other districts *(Moderate)*
Agua
Passeig Marítim 30
Olympic Village
Tel: 93 225 1272
Just beneath the giant goldfish, one of the few stylish places serving good food on the beach. Sought-after, so book. €

Casa Joana
Major de Sarrià 59
Sarrià
Tel: 93 203 1036
Checked tablecloths and home cooking (delicious *canelons* and braised veal) in this old 'village' restaurant. €

Above: Els Quatre Gats

NIGHTLIFE

'One morning I was awakened at four by loud conversation; going out on my balcony and looking down, I perceived that the rambla was still full of people sitting at café tables or on seats beneath trees, or strolling to and fro, talking, laughing and screaming with the greatest vivacity, the street lights that gleamed above the plane trees now paling a little in a faint dawn... It was a pretty and fantastic sight, this crowd bewitched into perpetual nocturnal animation.'

Rose Macaulay was writing in 1949, and though the Rambla today is not like that every night, *barcelonins*, like all Spaniards,

have an extraordinary capacity to stay up late. The working day doesn't end until 8pm, which means that nobody sits down to eat until around 10pm, so most entertainments don't begin until after that.

Nightclubs warm up from 2am and when they close around 5am people move on to *Afters*, bars that stay open till mid-morning. The real die-hards find places they can dance all day long, but it can cause havoc to your work schedule. The late-night crowds build up from Thursday through to Saturday.

Concerts, theatre, cinema

The main classical music venues are the **Palau de la Música Catalana**, the **Audi-**

tori in Glòries and the **Gran Teatre del Liceu** on the Rambla. Watch out for music played in other imposing surroundings, such as the **Saló de Cent** in the town hall; **Sant Felip Neri** and **Santa Maria del Pi** in the Gothic quarter and **Santa Maria del Mar**, where jazz is also sometimes played.

In the summer there's often music in public parks and medieval squares. From July to September musical evenings are held on the atmospheric roof terrace of Gaudí's La Pedrera and the Fundació Joan Miró has a summer season of contemporary music.

The principle theatres are the **National Theatre** (TNC) near Plaça de les Glòries; **Poliorama**, Rambla 15; the picturesque **Tivoli**, with early 20th-century décor, which often has modern, international productions; the **Mercat de les Flors**, Carrer de Lleida 19, with various spaces; and its neighbour, the **Teatre Lliure**. The **Espai Escènic Joan Brossa**, Allada Vermell 13, in the Born, has interesting off-beat productions.

Original-language (V.O.) films are shown at various cinemas, including **Casablanca** (Passeig de Gràcia 115); **Renoir- Les Corts**, Eugeni d'Ors 12, is a bit out of the way but shows good films on six screens; the **Icaria Yelmo** in the Olympic Village has 15 screens, and just about every film you could hope for; the **Verdi** complex with 9 screens in Gràcia (Carrer Verdi 32) and the **Verdi Park** (Torrijos 49) are also great places for a drink or snack afterwards. Remember that most films don't start until around 10pm

There are regular rock concerts, open-air in the Olympic Stadium or inside the impressive Palau Sant Jordi and all over town at festival time. More intimate concerts take place in **Bikini** (Déu i Mata 105), **La Boîte**, a former jazz club (Av. Diagonal 447) and **Razzmatazz** in Poble Nou (Almogàveres 122). In the Grec summer arts festival, music features strongly. There is a Jazz Festival in the Autumn and a Festival of Ancient Music in April and May. Keep an eye on local listings for the latest.

Bars, clubs and discos

Every night from pre-dinner cocktail hour until dawn, bar-flies hop from one nightspot to another all over town. In competing for custom, bars offer an enormous variety of

Above: audience participation in a Paral.lel nightclub

ambiences and styles, with various cocktails of music and drink. The smoother, designer bars tend to be in uptown Eixample, like the cool **Nick Havanna** (Carrer Rosselló 208) – the original designer bar from the 1980s – or **Snooker** (Roger de Llúria 42), where you can have a game if you wish.

However, it is downtown Barri Gòtic that has become the place for the young and trendy, though it does have a range to suit all tastes: from traditional old bars such as **Portalón** (Carrer Banys Nous 20) where the wine comes from barrels to the classic cocktail bar **Boadas** (Tallers 1). The daughter of its founder still shakes a mean Dry Martini. In the narrow streets between the Plaça George Orwell and the Plaça Reial, a new 'latest bar' opens every other month, from grunge to 1970s vinyl to cool lounge bars. **Al Limón Negro** (Escudellers Blancs) is an example, as is **Oviso** (Pl. George Orwell), which has a popular terrace. In La Ribera, **El Born** (Passeig del Born 26) in an old fish store, is just one of many places mushrooming in the labyrinth of medieval streets. **El Xampanyet**, serving its own *Cava* in Carrer de Montcada is worth a detour, though visitors to the Picasso museum will have got there first. Jazz fans might head for the **London Bar** (Nou de la Rambla 34), the **Jamboree** (Plaça Reial), or the **Harlem** (Comtessa de Sobradiel).

Nightclubs differ from bars in that they have an entrance fee (which will probably include the first drink). Again, they range from traditional discos to dance spaces with in-house or imported DJs, to classic dance halls. In **La Paloma** (Tigre 27; Thur–Sun) local couples dance regularly at afternoon sessions, as they have for the past 50 years, an experience not to be missed. Later on the band do salsa and after 3am the DJs move in with a hip new crowd. The **Torres de Avila** in the Poble Espanyol is visited for its design by Mariscal and Arribas more than its atmosphere.

Toilets are a point of style: at **Velvet** (Carrer de Balmes 161) men use a huge trough; at **Rosebud** in Tibidabo the doors to the men's and women's facilities lead to the same place.

Nightclubs and discos are usually quiet until well after midnight (although if you don't follow the crowd you might get the idea that some of them never get going at all). **KGB** in Carrer d'Alegre de Dalt 55 is a long-standing favourite, as is **Otto Zutz**, Carrer de Lincoln 15, one of the original designer discos that sometimes has live music. Newer on the scene is **Fellini**, La Rambla 27, a disco-lounge with several spaces playing different music. One of several clubs in the Vila Olímpica is CDLC – Carpe Diem Lounge Club, Passeig Marítim 32, where you can eat before the visiting DJs arrive.

When the party's finally over a dawn breakfast of chocolate and *churros* is inviting, at somewhere like **Vall d'Ouro**, Carrer Paris 198, off the Diagonal. It serves breakfast from 5am.

Flamenco, not a Catalan dance, has been increasing in popularity recently. A typical place to see it is **El Patio Andaluz** (Carrer d'Aribau 242; dinner or drink and show), or **Los Tarantos** (Plaça Reial 17). For cabaret acts delve into the Barri Xinés, between La Rambla and along Paral.lel, still, but only just, the seedy part of town.

There are very few music halls left. **Barcelona City Hall** (Rambla de Catalunya 2–4°) is a new-style music hall with regular shows. The **Apolo** (Nou de la Rambla 113) has become a trendy club with dance music and live concerts. And for those who want a flutter the **Gran Casino de Barcelona** is in the Olympic port, a far cry from the trendy night life in the Old Town.

Right: getting in the party mood

CALENDAR OF EVENTS

'The Catalans are the best innkeepers in Spain, and among the least bad cooks; and, although rude, unsocial and unfriendly to strangers, the Barcelonese among themselves are fond of gaity, feasting and masking.' The English travel writer Richard Ford never let courtesy muddy his prose.

'Masquerading is almost of absolute necessity to Spaniards,' he went on in his 1845 *Handbook for Travellers to Spain*, 'and especially to the intelligent Catalonians, whose capital is the head-quarters of the mask.'

The people of Barcelona today still like feasting and masking. These are wild and boisterous, but not usually drunken, occasions. Celebrations are held on the eve of the feasts, and last till dawn. The larger ones go on for several days.

Under Franco's dictatorship, pre-Lent **carnival** was banned in Catalonia from 1936 to 1980 but has since resurfaced as a spectacular event, most particularly in Sitges, a small town just south of the city, where a solid gay contingent in the processions always draws great applause.

At carnival straight men often dress as

women, too, and masked balls are held all over the town. If you are in Barcelona's Boqueria market (on the Rambla) at carnival time you will see stallholders entering into the spirit of the occasion, wearing masks or costumes as they serve their customers.

After carnival things are relatively quiet until the explosive celebration on the eve of the Feast of St John, **Sant Joan**, on 24 June. As in many other countries in Europe this is traditionally a night of midsummer bonfires, an ancient ritual with pagan origins that was adopted and adapted by the Christian church.

In Barcelona and the rest of Catalonia it is particularly joyous and greeted as the beginning of summer, even though the weather has warmed up before then. For several days leading up to it little boys throw fireworks annoyingly about the streets, and though there are some beautiful firework displays on the night, it can also be deafening. *Cava* is drunk and *coca* bread is eaten.

Each local quarter, or *barri*, has its own festival; some are confined to a street, others to wider areas. One of the best and most atmospheric is in the **Gràcia** *barri*. This one lasts for a week in August when the city is otherwise quite quiet. It attracts some good bands as well as turning out its *drac* (dragon), *gegants* (giants) and *dimonis* (devils).

However, the fiesta to end all fiestas is Barcelona's own **Festa Major** centred around the city's patron saint, La Mercè, whose winged figure flies on the skyline over her church behind the Passeig de Colom. Her feast day is on 24 September and in the **Setmana Gran** (the Big Week) there is a whole week of masking, dancing and feasting, with particularly fiery dragons and devils chasing people through the streets, the whole thing culminating in firework displays and bonfires.

Nationalist festivals

The more sober nationalist festivals are times for putting out the red-and-yellow striped Catalan flag. St George is Catalonia's patron saint and on his day, **Sant Jordi**, 23 April, bookstalls are set up in the Plaça Sant Jaume and throughout the city. Alongside them, single red roses are sold to men and boys who do not seem the least embarrassed

Left: the *castellers'* human towers are an integral part of many festivals

to buy them and carry them home through the streets for their mothers, girlfriends, mistresses and wives.

The book connection has less to do with St George than with the fact that 23 April is the anniversary of the death (in 1616) of Miguel de Cervantes (author of *Don Quixote*). William Shakespeare was born and died on the same date, and it has now been named World Book Day, in honour of the two great men.

The **Diada de Catalunya** on 11 September is an extremely sober occasion. This is the national day that commemorates the banning of the Catalan language and the loss of many ancient rights to Madrid, after troops led by the Bourbon king Felipe V captured Barcelona in 1713 following a devastating 13-month siege.

For obvious political reasons, the Diada was banned under Franco's regime but re-emerged after his death as a day of demonstrations and political activity.

Religious festivals are not celebrated here as elaborately as in many other parts of Spain. Christmas is preceded by the **Santa Llúcia** fair around the cathedral, selling decorations, gifts and everything you need to set the nativity scene. On a crisp winter day, with the smell of roast chestnuts in the air, it's a most enjoyable and festive occasion.

Christmas day itself is a family affair with a big get-together and blow-out meals on Boxing Day. New Year is celebrated with parties and dances, much as it is elsewhere in Europe. One national custom is to eat a grape and drink a sip of champagne on every stroke of the midnight hour, to ensure good luck throughout the year. Children look forward to the Three Kings, **Reis Mags**, on 6 January (Epiphany), for this is the day they customarily receive their presents. The kings arrive in the port by boat the night before and tour the streets giving out sweets.

Easter is heralded by religious processions during Holy Week, albeit far less devout than they used to be – and still are in some parts of Spain. Children only have a few days' holiday from school, and many people use the long weekend to get out of the city to the coast and the countryside.

The major festivals will have dancing giants and some will also have *castellers*, human towers that try to break records as the crowd pushes them onwards and upwards. There will also, more often than not, be a *sardana*, Catalonia's national dance, in which people hold hands in replicating circles. The 11-man band, called a *cobla*, plays on brass and wind instruments. They can otherwise be seen and heard outside the cathedral at noon on Sunday.

Above: giants in the Plaça Sant Jaume on the feast of La Mercè

Practical Information

GETTING THERE

By Air

Barcelona airport (tel: 93 298 38 38) is about 12km (7 miles) south of the city at El Prat. Iberia is the country's national carrier and there is a shuttle service from here to the capital, Madrid.

The airport is equipped with tourist offices, banks, car-hire facilities and a hotel reservation service. Trains leave for the city every 30 minutes for Sants (about 20 minutes) and Plaça Catalunya. The excellent Aerobus leaves for Plaça Catalunya every 12 minutes and costs around 3€. Taxis cost around 18€.

The main airlines have offices in the city. Iberia's office is at Diputació 258. For international reservations and information, tel: 902 400 500.

By Road

The French border is 149km (92 miles) north at La Jonquera on the A7 motorway. The toll amounts to around 10€. Avoid Friday night and Sunday evening rush-hours. The Royal Automobile Club of Catalunya (RACC) is manned 24 hours. It is at Avinguda Diagonal, 687, Barcelona 08028; tel: 93 495 5000/900 365 505 (244).

By Rail

The main RENFE stations are Estació de França which is by the port, and Sants, which is towards the south. But many trains go through the city. If they do, it may well be more convenient to disembark at Passeig de Gràcia or Plaça de Catalunya. For all rail enquiries, tel: 902 240 202 (national), 902 24 3 402 (international).

By Sea

Trasmediterranea has a regular ferry service to the Balearic islands (tel: 902 454 645). Grimaldi Ferries run a daily service to Civitavecchia (for Rome) (tel: 93 502 8163).

Left: getting a great view of the city

When to Go

Average winter temperatures are 54°F (12°C), summers 75°F (24°C). Winter evenings can be chilly but the sun can shine, too. Easter and autumn are mild and pleasant. Schools break up for the summer around 24 June and by August the city is so humid that some 60 percent of businesses close down for the month, which makes it delightfully empty, but also sometimes frustrating. People dress well in the city, whatever the weather.

TRAVEL ESSENTIALS

Passports

Passports are required by all non-Spaniards. It's a good idea to have a photocopy of the relevant pages, which saves taking the real thing everywhere. You need ID in order to pay with a credit card.

Tourist Offices abroad:

Australia: Level 2
203 Castlereagh Street
PO Box A-685
Sydney NSW 2000
Tel: 2 9264 7966; fax: 2 9267 5111.

Canada: 34th Floor
2 Bloor Street West
Toronto, Ontario M4W 3E2.
Tel: 416 961 3131; fax: 416 961 1992.

UK: 79 New Cavendish Street
London W1W 6XB.
Tel: 0207 486 8077; fax: 0207 486 8034
Brochure line: 08459 400 180.

USA: Floor 35
666 Fifth Avenue
New York, NY 10103
Tel: 212 265 8822; fax: 212 265 88 64.

Consulates in Barcelona
Australia   tel: 93 490 9013
Canada   tel: 93 204 2700
Ireland   tel: 93 491 5021
UK   tel: 93 366 6200
USA   tel: 93 280 2227

Health
Water is drinkable but can taste unpleasant
because of the purifying salts used. Mineral
water is readily available (*agua con gas* is
sparkling, *sin gas* is still). A chemist (*far-
màcia*) is the best place to go for minor ail-
ments. UK citizens with an E111 form
(available from UK post offices: since 2005
each member of the family must have his
or her own form) are entitled to to recipro-
cal health facilities, but to cover all even-
tualities private insurance is recommended.

Time Zones
Spain is one hour ahead of Greenwich Mean
Time (Eastern Standard Time + 6 hrs) in win-
ter; two in summer.

USEFUL INFORMATION

Money
The currency is the euro (€). Travellers'
cheques are widely accepted. Bank hours are
usually 8.30am–2pm Monday to Friday. Major credit cards are accepted and most banks
have cash points. For American Express tel:
902 375 637; Visa 900 991 216; MasterCard
900 971 1231.

Business Hours
Hours vary, but most shops and businesses open 9am–2pm and 4–8pm.
Many public bodies work straight
through from 8am–3pm, a particularly
popular work schedule in summer.

Holidays
The city closes down on public holidays and
many people leave town, particularly if they
can snatch another day – known as a *puente*,
or bridge – between the day off and the weekend. Christmas is not such an occasion as it
is in northern Europe and school holidays
then, and at Easter, are short.

1 January	New Year
6 January	Epiphany/Els Reis
Good Friday	
Easter Monday	
1 May	Festa de Treball
24 June	Sant Joan, Midsummer's Day
15 August	Feast of the Assumption
11 September	La Diada: Catalan National Day
24 September	La Mercè festival
12 October	Hispanitat, Spanish National Day
1 November	All Saints
6 December	Constitució, Constitution Day
8 December	Immaculate Conception
25 December	Christmas Day
26 December	St Stephen's Day

Religious Services
Catholic: Paroisse Françoise (in French and
English), Anglí 15, tel: 93 204 49 62. **An-
glican**: St George's Church, Sant Joan de
la Salle, 41, tel: 93 417 88 67. **Jewish**: Sinagoga de la Comunidad Judia, Avenir 24,
tel: 93 200 61 48. **Islamic**: Toarek Ben Ziad,
Hospital 91, tel: 93 441 91 49.

LANGUAGE

Although Catalan is the local language, so
many people from other parts of Spain live
in Barcelona that Castilian (Spanish) is also
used. Here are some helpful Catalan and
Spanish phrases:

English	Catalan/Spanish
Good morning	Bon dia/ Buenos dias
Good afternoon	Bona tarda/ Buenas tardes

EMERGENCIES

Crime
In any city, tourists are a target for pick-pockets and muggers. Only carry what you are likely to need. Never leave valuables in your car, always wear cameras and bags with their straps securely across your chest, and avoid the narrow Old Town streets at night.

In case of theft, assault or loss contact the Autonomous Police (Mossos d'Esquadia) (088), City Police (092), or 112, a general emergency number with a multilingual service. It is essential that you make a statement *(denuncia)* at a police station (e.g. in Nou de la Rambla 80 or in the metro of Plaça Catalunya) in case of passport loss or to make an insurance claim. The Guardia Urbana at La Rambla 43 are always helpful.

Medical Help
In cases of emergency go directly to the *urgències* (accident) departments at any of these hospitals: Hospital Sant Pau, Carrer Sant Antoni María Claret 167 (tel: 436 47 11), or Hospital Clínic, Carrer Villarroel, 170 (tel: 93 227 5400).
Dentist: Clínica Janos, Carrer de Muntaner 375 6º 2ª, (tel: 93 200 2333). Open daily 8am–1.30pm, 4–8.30pm.

Emergency Numbers
General: 112
Fire Brigade: 080
Ambulance Service: 061
City Police: 092
Lost Property: 010

COMMUNICATIONS & MEDIA

Telephone
Phone booths take coins and phone cards (available at *estancos* or post offices), with the latter being the most suitable for calls abroad. Some phone booths also take credit cards. It can be easier to phone first and pay later in one of the privately run telephone exchanges. However, beware of the bill, as rates are high.

To dial Barcelona from abroad use the code for Spain (34) followed by that for

English	Catalan/Spanish
Good night:	Bona nit/ Buenas noches
Goodbye	Adeu/Adios
Please	Si us plau/ Por favor
Thank you	Gracies/ Gracias
Where is...?	On es...?/ Donde esta...?
How much is it?	Quant val?/ Cuanto es?
one	un(a)/uno
two	dos (dues)/dos
three	tres/tres
four	quatre/cuatro
five	cinc/cinco
six	sis/seis
seven	set/siete
eight	vuit/ocho
nine	nou/nueve
ten	deu/diez
Do you have a room for night?	Té una habitació per una nit/Tiene una habitación para una noche?
Open	Obert/Abierto
Closed	Tancat/Cerrado
Today	Avui/Hoy
Tomorrow	Demà/Mañana
Yesterday	Ahir/Ayer

Left: there are plenty of opportunities to change money in the city
Above: Barcelona's distinctive phone boxes are usually in good working order

Barcelona (93). From anywhere in Spain and in the city itself, Barcelona numbers begin with 93. From Barcelona, the international operator service for Europe is 1008, for the rest of the world 1005.

To call other countries, first dial the international access code 00, then the relevant country code: Australia (61); France (33); Germany (49); Italy (39); Japan (81); Netherlands (31); UK (44); US and Canada (1). If you are using a credit phone card, dial the company's access number below, then 01, and then the country code. AT&T, tel: 900 990 011; Interglobe, tel: 900 974 479; MCI, tel: 900 990 014; Sprint, tel: 900 990 013.

Post Offices
The main post office is in Plaça Antoni Lopez near the port, open 9am–9pm Monday to Friday, 9am–2pm Saturday. Other post offices *(correu)* are open in the mornings only. Stamps can be bought at tobacconists *(tabacs)*, which have brown and yellow signs.

Internet Connections
There are no end of places now available for checking your e-mail: on La Rambla and off it, in hotels and in cafés. For example, there's EasyEverything Ronda Universitat 35, another star product from the Easy family, promising the fastest Internet connections. Open 24 hours, 7 days a week, with 300 computers. There's not much of a refreshment service, but still they're queuing. In a quiet street near the Picasso Museum Bornet, Barra de Ferro, 3 is like a small attractive club. Open until 10pm daily.

Media
Barcelona's daily papers are *La Vanguardia*, *El Periodico* (published in Spanish and Catalan) and *Avui* (Catalan). The national *El Pais* has a Barcelona edition. All of them cover events in the city. *Guía del Ocio* is the local weekly listings magazine, with good coverage of what's on in town. *Metropolitan*, a useful free English monthly is available in the Palau de la Virreina (La Rambla 99) and from some bars and bookshops. *Catalonia Today* is a weekly English paper.

GETTING AROUND

A car is unnecessary in Barcelona, which has buses and a good Metro system. A map of the city is essential. These are supplied by the tourist offices, who continually update their information pamphlets.

Tourist Information Offices
The main Barcelona tourist office is beneath Plaça Catalunya (near Portal del Angel; 9am–9pm daily). It's fully equipped with exchange facilities, hotel booking and internet services.

Other tourist offices are to be found in Sants Station (8am–8pm, winter weekends 8am–2pm); in the Town Hall (Plaça Sant Jaume; 10am–8pm; Sunday 10am–2pm; www.bcn.es); and at Barcelona airport (9am–7pm; Saturday 9am–2pm; closed Sunday; Terminal A, tel: 93 478 4704; Terminal B, tel: 93 478 0565).

For tourist information on Catalonia go to Palau Robert, Passeig de Gràcia, 107 (10am–7pm; Sunday 10am–2pm; tel: 93 238 4000; www.gencat.es/probert).

Left Luggage
There are left luggage lockers at França, Sants and Passeig de Gràcia stations and at the Maritime station on the Moll de Barcelona. There is also storage in the Barcelona Nord bus station.

Metro
There are six colour-coded Metro lines, which are numbered 1–5 and 11. Tickets are inexpensive and it's worth buying a T-10 card (to get 10 journeys for the price of five

Left: catching up with the news at a newsstand on La Rambla

and a half), which can also be used on the buses and FGC line. Transfers from the Metro to a bus or train are not charged if done within 90 minutes.

FGC AND RENFE

Ferrocarrils de la Generalitat de Catalunya (FGC) are similar to the Metro but extend inland to Sarrià, Tibidabo and Reina Elisenda towards the Collserola hills. They run from Plaça Catalunya, and go beyond the hill to Terrassa and Sabadell. The FGC line at Plaça d'Espanya goes to Manresa, Igualada and Montserrat. Rodalies Renfe goes from Plaça Catalunya to Vilafranca and the Maresme coast.

Bus

Bus lanes make journeys nearly as swift as the Metro. All night services (Nitbus) pass through Plaça Catalunya.

Tram

A new tram service connects the Olympic Village to Diagonal Mar and beyond. It also runs on the Diagonal above Plaça Francesc Macià. The T-10 is valid on the trams.

Taxi

Black-and-yellow Barcelona taxis are not expensive. The standard fare varies according to the time of day and whether it's a weekend or not. A small tip is always appreciated. Luggage costs extra.

Above: ascending Tibidabo by funicular

CITY PARKS

The *espais urbans* (urban spaces) are planned havens scattered around the city: for example, in front of the main RENFE station Sants (Metro lines 3 and 5), is the Plaça Països Catalans, and nearby is the much-photographed **Parc de l'Espanya Industrial**, which was designed by the Basque architect Luis Peña Ganchegui on the site of a former textile factory. Centred on a large lake where rowing boats can be hired, the 5-ha (12-acre) space is dominated by 10 futuristic watch towers.

The **Parc Joan Miró**, in Carrer d'Aragó, is well signposted by the artist's towering 22-m (70-ft) colourful mosaic-covered sculpture *Dona i Ocell* (Woman and Bird). The park is on two levels and occupies a former slaughterhouse, which gives it its other name, Parc de l'Escorxador. The sculpture rises from a small pond in the upper level; the lower level has palm-lined avenues brightened by oleander.

Formal gardens are not generally a feature of the city, but one pleasant example is the **Parc del Laberint de Horta** located behind the Velòdrom cycle track in the Vall d'Hebron, on the northwestern edge of the city and set against the heights of the Serra de Collserola.

The Velòdrom is on the inland side of the Passeig de la Vall d'Hebron, part of the city's new ring road, reached from the new Metro

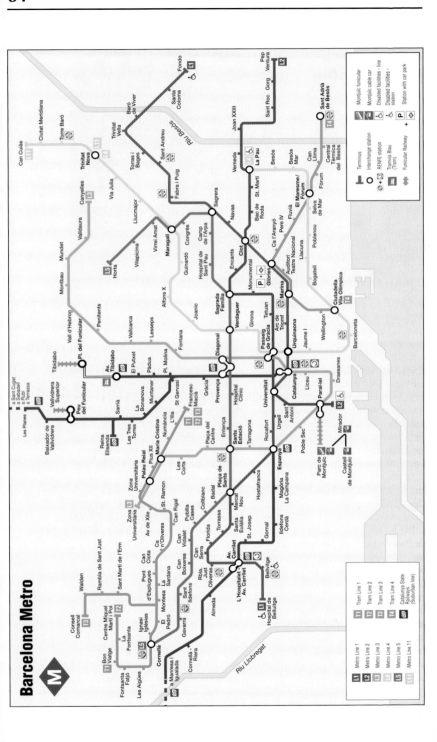

Barcelona Metro

stop, Mundet, on Metro line 3. It is easily identified by the gas spheres up above it, which look very similar to two great eyeballs keeping watch over the city. On the far side a footbridge has been incorporated to take pedestrians directly to the Laberint park. The whole place is the inspiration of the Marqués of Alfarres, who early last century had a neo-Islamic mansion built around a medieval tower.

To the right of it, approached from the rear, is the attractive walled **Patí de les Carmelites** (daily 10am–2pm) offering topiaried walks, yuccas and tall palms.

Nearby, and entirely different in style is the **Parc de la Creueta del Coll**. Three stops back down the Metro line to Penitents, just below the sports complex built for the Olympics, this bright new public space was created in a disused quarry by Joan Martorell and David Mackay, two local architects. Among its various attractions is an outdoor swimming pool complete with a sandy beach and the *Elogi de l'Aigua* (Water Eulogy) sculpture by Eduardo Chillida suspended overhead.

The third park in this area, just below the Creueta del Coll, is perhaps the best known of Barcelona's parks because of its *Modernista* architect: this is Gaudí's **Park Güell** (*see Itinerary 3, page 34*).

ACCOMMODATION

There is a wide choice of good hotels in the city, and more are being built all the time. It is essential to book in advance, not just during the tourist season, but any time of year, on account of the number of trade fairs and conventions that are held in the city, as well as increasing tourism.

Prices range from around 150–over 300 euros for a double room in a five-star hotel to approximately 45–75 euros in a pleasant small hotel: however, the star system is not necessarily an accurate indication of price. In general, the more modestly priced hotels and hostels are situated downtown. Head for the streets off the Rambla if you are looking for bargain *pensions*.

In the Eixample
Claris Gran Luxe★★★★★
Pau Claris 150, 08009
Tel: 93 487 6262
Fax: 93 215 7970
Latter-day luxuries and ancient art in the smooth modern interior built behind the façade of the 19th-century Palau Vedruna, where you can even rent 'house' mopeds to whiz around town.

Avenida Palace★★★★
Gran Via de les Corts Catalanes 605, 08007
Tel: 93 301 9600
Fax: 93 318 1234
This is an old-fashioned gilded palace which was formerly a cinema, and is frequently recommended.

Condes de Barcelona★★★★
Passeig de Gràcia 75, 08008
Tel: 93 467 4780
Fax: 93 467 4785
Occupying an attractive *Modernista* building, the Condes de Barcelona has great character and is set in a wonderful location.

Ducs de Bergara★★★★
Carrer de Bergara 11, 08002
Tel: 93 301 5151
Fax: 93 317 3442
Located just off Plaça de Catalunya, this hotel occupies a fine *fin-de-siècle* mansion and has a delightfully personal atmosphere.

Above: the Old Town is the best bet for inexpensive accommodation

Gallery★★★★
Carrer Rosselló 249, 08008
Tel: 93 415 9911
Fax: 93 415 9184
In heart of the Eixample with all mod cons, this efficient but friendly hotel has the added bonus of a peaceful and attractive garden at the rear. Request a room looking on to it when you make your reservation.

Gran Hotel Havana★★★★
Gran Via de les Corts Catalanes 647, 08010
Tel: 93 412 1115
Fax: 93 412 2611
The Gran Hotel Havana has a serene and elegant modern interior behind a traditional Eixample facade, filled with light from a spectacular glass atrium. The rooms are pleasant if rather on the small side, and the staff are affable.

Majestic★★★★
Passeig de Gràcia 70, 08007
Tel: 93 488 1717
Fax: 93 488 1880
True to its name this revamped large hotel right in the centre of the Eixample is now extremely sophisticated with a highly acclaimed restaurant, the Drolma.

Granvia★★★
Gran Via de les Corts Catalanes 642, 08007
Tel: 93 318 1900
Fax: 93 318 9997
This older-style hotel has a great location close to the Passeig de Gràcia and offers plenty of personality. It also represents excellent value.

Neutral★★
Rambla de Catalunya 42, 08007
Tel: 93 487 6390
Fax: 93 487 4028
Comfortable hotel which offers reasonable value. For great views, ask for a balcony overlooking the street.

Windsor★★
Rambla de Catalunya 84, 08008
Tel: 93 215 1198
Bright, clean and very well situated.

Hostal Ciudad Condal
Carrer Mallorca 255, 08008
Tel: 93 215 1040
Shortcomings in interior décor easily compensated by central location in this acceptable, well-positioned *pension*.

San Medin
Gran de Gràcia 125, 08012
Tel: 93 217 3068
A comfortable little *pension* at the top end of the Passeig de Gràcia.

Seafront and Ciutadella
Arts Hotel★★★★★
Passeig de la Marina 19
Tel: 93 221 1000
Fax: 93 221 1070
A high-rise hotel with a very high profile, it stands by the beach and marks the entrance to the Olympic Village. Every comfort plus panoramic views.

Park★★★
Avinguda Marquès de l'Argentera 11, 08003
Tel: 93 319 6000
Fax: 93 319 4519
Wonderful period-piece from the 1950s, carefully restored in 1990, this is a great hotel, ideal for El Born nightlife and access to beach. Very good value.

Triunfo★★
Passeig de Picasso 22
Tel: 93 315 0860
Fax: 93 315 0860
The Triunfo is a simple, basic but very clean little *pension* situated, like the Park Hotel, conveniently close to Ciutadella and El Born's attractions

Above: the Hotel Suizo has a tempting *pasteleria* next door

practical information

The Old Town

Le Meridien★★★★★
Rambla 111, 08002
Tel: 93 318 6200
Fax: 93 301 7776
An old building that has been brought up-to-date with modern facilities including personal computers.

Albinoni★★★
Avinguda Portal de l'Angel 17, 08002
Tel: 93 318 4141
Fax: 93 301 2631
A newcomer in the Old Town. This 19th-century palace has been well renovated to become an attractive modern hotel while retaining many original decorative features. There are peaceful rooms at the back with small terraces.

Colón★★★★
Avinguda de Catedral 7, 08002
Tel: 93 301 1404
Fax: 93 317 2915
The Colón is one of the city's best-known hotels. Facing the cathedral, it is an extremely comfortable place with a relaxed, old-world feel.

Continental★★★
La Rambla 138, 08002
Tel: 93 301 2570
Fax: 93 302 7360

Featured in Orwell's *Homage to Catalonia* – which is enough to attract many people – this is an eccentric hotel fully carpeted and wallpapered, but its individuality has charm and the rooms on La Rambla are in a prime position. All round good value.

Oriente★★★
Rambla 45–47, 08002
Tel: 93 302 2558
Fax: 93 412 3819
Built around a 17th-century monastic college, the Oriente has been a hotel for over a century. Good-sized rooms.

San Agustí★★★
Plaça de Sant Agustí 3, 08001
Tel: 93 318 1658
Fax: 93 317 2928
Attractive hotel in a pretty square off La Rambla. The best rooms are under the beams on the fourth floor and are well worth the extra cost.

España★★
Carrer de Sant Pau 9–11, 08001
Tel: 93 318 1758
Fax: 93 317 1134
This hotel has a beautiful Domènech i Montaner dining room, but unfortunately this is not matched by the bedrooms. The set menu lunch, amid the Modernist decor, is very good value.

Above: the state-of-the-art Arts Hotel

Hosteria Grau★★
Ramelleres, 27, 08001
Tel: 93 301 8135
Fax: 93 317 6825
On the basic side, but simple, clean and very reasonable. Only 5 minutes from airport bus terminal in Plaça de Catalunya and convenient for all parts of town.

Jardi★★
Sant Josep Oriol 1, 08002
Tel: 93 301 5900
Fax: 93 318 3664
One of the best-situated of the small hotels, the Jardí is also relatively inexpensive. Word has got around, so book early; ask for a room with a balcony.

Nouvel★★★
Santa Ana 18–20, 08002
Tel: 93 301 8274
Fax: 93 301 8370
The Nouvel offers pleasant art nouveau surroundings. Just off the Rambla.

Rialto★★
Carrer Ferrán 42
Tel: 93 318 5212
Fax: 93 38 5312
No frills but comfortable and clean in a pleasant street near Plaça Sant Jaume.

Peninsular★
Carrer de Sant Pau 34, 08001
Tel: 302 3138
Fax: 412 3699
Set in a former Augustinian monastery, with an attractive internal courtyard. Good value with lots of character and obliging staff.

Self Catering
Self-catering is a popular option with many flats available for short rentals, mostly in the Old Town, or Apart-hotels such as:
Access
Gran Via de les Corts Catalans
Tel: 93 425 5161
Bertrán
Carrer Bertrán 150
Tel: 93 212 7550
Senator
Via Augusta 167
Tel: 93 201 1405

Central Booking
If you have trouble finding a hotel – and rooms do get booked well in advance – you could try contacting the Tourist Office booking service in the Plaça Catalunya, tel: 93 285 3833:
Derby Hotels
Tel: 93 414 2970
Guitart Hotels
Tel: 97 234 7000
Hoteles Catalonia
Tel: 93 418 4818
NH Hotels
Tel: 93 412 2323

FURTHER READING

Barcelona, Robert Hughes. HarperCollins. An fullsome appraisal of the city and its culture by *Time* magazine's art critic.
Barcelona Design Guide. Editorial Gustavo Gili SA. A handy pocket book giving the low-down on the city's centre for good design and the more stylish nightclubs, interiors, and shopping in general.
Barcelona: a Thousand Years of the City's Past, Felipe Fernandez-Armesto. Oxford University Press. A detailed and provocative view of the city by a non-Catalan.
Catalan Cuisine, Colman Andrews. Headline. A lively and intelligent account of the region's food.
Forbidden Territory, Juan Goytisolo. Quartet Books. An autobiography that gives great insight into the city during the years of Franco's dictatorship.
Gaudi: A Biography, Gijs van Hensbergen. HarperCollins. One of the more recent attempts to captutre the architect's life.
Homage to Barcelona, Colm Toíbín. Simon & Schuster. An excellent award-winning account by this gifted Irish writer.
Insight Guides, from Apa Publications, has Barcelona titles in all its series as well as this Pocket Guide. Insight City Guides, Insight Compact Guides and Insight Berlitz Guide are renowned for the quality of their photographs, excellent maps and information on history and culture. They also have titles on many other Spanish destinations, including several of its many regions. *Insight Guide: Spain* covers the whole country.

Right: a leisurely way to view the city's sights

ACKNOWLEDGEMENTS

Photography	**Annabel Elston** *and*
13	**AKG**
2/3	**J. D. Dallet**
7B, 27	**Jerry Dennis**
78	**Wolfgang Fritz**
45	**Andrew Holt**
61, 72	**Tor Eigeland**
10	**Jose Martin**
42, 67	**Mike Merchant**
29T	**Ingrid Morato**
5, 14, 32, 36, 39, 47, 50, 56, 61, 62, 66, 73, 74, 75, 77, 87	**Prisma Archivo Fotografico**
11	**Jan Read**
16	**Topham Picturepoint**
22T, 25B, 26T/B, 30T, 34B, 35, 43, 52, 58, 59, 63, 64T, 68, 76, 85, 90	**Bill Wassman**
1, 8/9, 15, 38, 48, 53, 60, 69	**Roger Williams**
82	**George Wright**
29	**Gregory Wrona**
Cover	**Greg Balfour Evans**
Back Cover	**Annabel Elston**
Cartography	**Berndtson & Berndtson**

Left: the Magic Fountain casts its spell in front of the Palau Nacional

www.insightguides.com

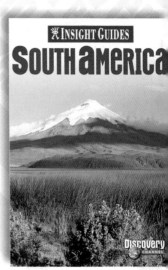

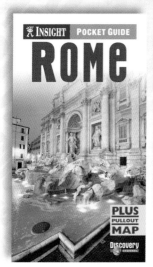
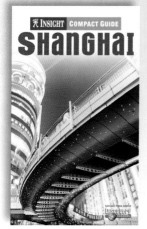

☀ INSIGHT GUIDES

The World Leader in Visual Travel Guides & Maps

As travellers become ever more discriminating, Insight Guides is using the vast experience gained over three-and-a-half decades of guidebook publishing to create an even wider range of titles to serve them. For those who want the big picture, Insight Guides and Insight City Guides provide comprehensive coverage of a destination. Insight Pocket Guides supply personal recommendations for a short stay. Insight Compact Guides are attractively portable. Insight FlexiMaps are both rugged and easy to use. And specialist titles cover shopping, eating out, and museums and galleries. Wherever you're going, our writers and photographers have already been there – more than once.

INDEX